2013 年度湖北省教育厅人文社会科学研究项目

（项目编号：13g548）

武当山英文导游辞研究与创作

张正荣　著

南开大学出版社

天　津

图书在版编目(CIP)数据

武当山英文导游辞研究与创作 / 张正荣著. 一天津：
南开大学出版社，2013.4
ISBN 978-7-310-04139-8

Ⅰ.①武… Ⅱ.①张… Ⅲ.①英语－导游－解说
词－写作②武当山－导游－解说词－写作 Ⅳ.①H315
②K928.3

中国版本图书馆 CIP 数据核字(2013)第 059204 号

版权所有　侵权必究

南开大学出版社出版发行

出版人：孙克强

地址：天津市南开区卫津路 94 号　　邮政编码：300071
营销部电话：(022)23508339　23500755
营销部传真：(022)23508542　　邮购部电话：(022)23502200

*

河北昌黎太阳红彩色印刷有限责任公司印刷
全国各地新华书店经销

*

2013 年 4 月第 1 版　　2013 年 4 月第 1 次印刷
210×148 毫米　32 开本　5.5 印张　151 千字

定价：30.00 元

如遇图书印装质量问题，请与本社营销部联系调换，电话：(022)23507125

序

武当山是中国著名的道教圣地。鲁迅先生说过:"中国的根底在道教。"如何更好地宣传武当、宣传中国文化是每一位同仁义不容辞的责任。

张正荣副教授自2005年起,对武当文化及中西文化差异进行了深入的研究。其新作《武当山英文导游辞研究与创作》即将出版,本人有幸先睹为快,快读之余,感到张正荣副教授的新作内容丰富,不仅填补了武当山英文导游辞研究与创作的空白,而且为英美人了解当今中国社会,了解武当山开辟了新的途径。

本书的特点为:

(1)针对性:本书作者针对不同类型的游客,如一般观光型游客、文化需求型游客、来自北京的游客以及游玩期间是雨天的游客,提供了不同风格的武当山简介,避免了千篇一律、陈词滥调。

(2)知识性:知识层次相对较高,有较强求知欲的游客,他们对导游讲解要求也相对较高。这样的讲解很容易与旅游者发生互动,产生共鸣。当面对金碧辉煌的武当山金殿时,本书作者不仅介绍了康熙书写"金光妙相"的背景,而且讲述了中国古建、风水知识。在武当山简介中,作者提到明朝两位皇帝明成祖朱棣和明世宗朱厚熜,这些可使外国游客对武当山有更好的了解。

(3)跨文化性:"跨文化性"是国际旅游中导游工作的特点之

一。因为涉外导游是在各种文化的差异中工作，所以应具备跨文化意识、跨文化知识、跨文化思维等。如本书作者在讲解桂花时，详解了桂花在中西方文化中所产生的不同联想及含义。又如"三清"为道教最高神，很多导游可能不知道如何表达，采用直译"sanqing"，结果游客丈二和尚摸不着头脑，不知所云。该书作者通过与外国游客的沟通，了解到"the Three Pure Ones"能使外国游客一听便知，起到很好的交流作用。

（4）趣味性：增强讲解的趣味性，提高游客的游兴，是每位涉外导游追求的一种境界。要在导游讲解时显得幽默，只能从提高自身素养，增长自身见识入手。本书作者在一雌一雄两个狮子前（雌狮爪子下有一个小狮子，而雄狮爪子下有一个圆球），指着这对狮子对旅游者说："Look, this male lion is carefree, he is playing football all day long, but his wife has to take care of the baby all by herself"，不乏幽默感。

（5）实用性。目前关于武当山的网络和纸质的英文资料不多。可喜的是一些学者已开始关注这个问题，并进行了一些有益的尝试。在少量的资料中，我们发现存在一些问题，如直接把中文导游辞一句一句地翻译，全然不考虑中西文化差异及英文导游辞的特点。如一本有关武当山的导游书，对"始判六天"如此解释："It means the Taoist first distinguishes the universe has six layers and then have 33 Heavens and 36 Heavens. The highest layer is called Daluo Heaven; the holy day is the San Qing Heaven." 作者想表达的意思为"道教最先辨别断定宇宙为六重天，其后才有三十三天、三十六天之说，称最高为大罗天，最圣为三清天。"这段话对于中国游客都显得很晦涩，外国游客听了更是云里雾里。该书作者因具带团经验，所以能更好地传播中国传统文化。

张正荣副教授是我多年的学生加好友，她兴趣广泛，视野开阔，在治学方面勤奋严谨。她很早就开始搜集武当山文化方面的材料，对武当山导游辞更是倍加关注，对武当文化与英美文化的异同进行了比较研究，在分析、整理收集到的资料的基础上，梳理思路，取精用弘，创作了《武当山英文导游辞研究与创作》。这部大作比较完整地讲述了武当山相关知识，同时考虑到文化的差异和英文导游辞的特点，集知识性与趣味性为一体，确实难能可贵。承蒙错爱，向予索序，却之不恭，凑得数语，得以交差。

值该书出版之际，谨表示衷心的祝贺！希望该书能引起同行的关注，不管是表扬，还是批评。目的只有一个，希望武当文化能在同行的努力下走得更远！发展得更好！希望中国的涉外导游的素质越来越高，中国传统文化传播得更广更深！

杨贤玉　教授、硕士生导师

湖北汽车工业学院外语系系主任

2012 年 8 月 1 日

Contents

I. A Brief Introduction to Wudang Mountain

1.1 The Introduction for Sightseers

First, the guide sings a song《天下太极出武当》（songwriter 宋晓明，composer 赵季平，singer 王宏伟），which is followed by the introduction:

Have you ever heard the song? It's about Wudang Mountain. Can you sing other songs about Wudang Mountain (The guide may also sing 《武当山歌》written by Li Faping, head of Wudang Mountain Tourism Economic Zone)? Now we are going to Wudang Mountain.

Wudang Mountain reached its peak in the Ming Dynasty. In order to have a better understanding of Wudang Mountain, we have to mention two emperors. One is Zhu Di and the other is Zhu Houcong. In 1399, Zhu Di seized the throne by force in the name of quelling so-called rebellions. He became Emperor Chengzu. In order to give a good name to his usurpation of the throne, Zhu Di claimed that what he had done was under Zhenwu's tacit permission, that he upheld justice on behalf of Zhenwu. In 1412, Zhu Di sent 300,000 soldiers and craftsmen to Wudang Mountain building Taoist temples, and chose famous Taoists from Taoist temples throughout the country to Wudang Mountain as chief Taoists. Zhu Houcong issued 140 imperial edicts to Wudang Mountain, the greatest number among all the emperors. Over the years, Zhu Houcong's devotion to Taoism became a heavy financial burden for the empire and created dissent across the country. Particularly during his later years, Zhu Houcong was known for spending a great deal of time on alchemy in hopes of finding medicines to prolong his life. He would recruit young girls in their early teens and engage in sexual activities in hope of empowering himself, along with the consumption of potent elixirs. He employed Taoist priests to collect rare minerals from all over the country to create elixirs, including elixirs containing mercury, which inevitably posed health problems at high doses (Refer to Zhu Houcong in Extended Reading 1 and Zhu Di in Celebrity Hall).

Do you know how Wudang Mountain get its name? We may separate the Chinese character "武" into two parts "止" and "戈". They mean stop fighting, so we should live in harmony with no fighting. In the Spring and Autumn and Warring States Periods, Wudang Mountain was located at the junction of Chu Kingdom, Qin Kingdom and Han Kingdom. For its strategic location, about 20 wars happened here and in the neighboring areas.

Wudang Mountain, just to the south of the city of Shiyan, Hubei Province, is one of the first groups of national key scenic spots; in 1994, the monasteries and buildings were made a UNESCO World Cultural Heritage Site.

Wudang Mountain spans an area of 312 square kilometers. Due to the mild climate and favorable position, Wudang Mountain is home to a great variety of plants and animals. Some of them are species of rare plants and animals on the brink of extinction. Wudang Mountain is the habitat for over 2,518 medical herbs，536 more than those recorded in *Compendium of Meteria Medica*（《本草纲目》）by Li Shizhen. So it enjoys the name of "Natural Medical Storehouse."

The overall landscape of Wudang Mountain can be described as the following: 72 peaks, 36 hanging rocks, 24 ravines, 10 pools, 9 palaces, 9 springs, 8 Taoist temples and 3 ponds.

The highest peak on Wudang Mountain is Tianzhu Peak（天柱峰）; it's 1,612 meters above sea level. It literally means a great pillar propping up the sky. From a distance, it looks like 72 Taoists making a pilgrimage to the Golden Hall, except one peak, named Jiangfeng Peak（犟峰）. Jiang in Chinese means "stubborn", that is to say the peak refuses to make a pilgrimage to the Golden Hall. It's also like a fire flame. On the top is Zhenwu, the god of water. So here comes the saying, "Fei Zhen Wu Bu Zu Dang Zhi", which means only Zhenwu enjoys the power and privilege to live here.

Wudang Mountain has four major scenic zones: Taizipo Palace (Crown Prince Palace), Zixiao Palace (Purple Heaven Palace), Nanyan Palace (Southern Crag Palace) and the Palace of Supreme Harmony. Let me introduce them for you one by one.

Extended Reading 1: The Jiajing Emperor (Zhu Houcong)

The Jiajing Emperor was the 11th Ming Dynasty Emperor of China who ruled from 1521 to 1567. Born Zhu Houcong, he was the former Emperor, Zhengde Emperor's cousin. As the nephew of the

Hongzhi Emperor, Zhu Houcong was not brought up to succeed to the throne. However, the throne became vacant in 1521 with the sudden death of the Hongzhi Emperor's son, Emperor Zhengde, who did not leave an heir. The 15-year-old Zhu Houcong was chosen to become emperor.

Custom dictated that an emperor who was not an immediate descendant of the previous one should be adopted by the previous one, to maintain an unbroken line. Such a posthumous adoption of Zhu Houcong by Emperor Zhengde was proposed, but he resisted, preferring instead to have his father declared emperor posthumously. This conflict is known as "The Great Rites Controversy（大礼仪之争）". The Jiajing Emperor prevailed, and hundreds of his opponents were banished, physically beaten in the court（廷杖）or executed.

The Jiajing Emperor was known to be a cruel and self-aggrandizing emperor and he also chose to reside outside of the Forbidden City in Beijing so he could live in isolation. Jiajing also abandoned the practice of seeing his ministers altogether from 1539 onward and for a period of almost 25 years refused to give official audiences, relaying his wishes through eunuchs and officials.

Jiajing's ruthlessness also led to an internal plot—the Palace Coup in the Year Renyin（壬寅宫变）by his concubines to assassinate him in October, 1542 by strangling him while he slept. A group of palace girls who had had enough of Jiajing's cruelty decided to band together to murder the emperor. The leading palace girl tried to strangle the emperor with ribbons from her hair while the others held down the emperor's arms and legs but made a fatal mistake by tying a knot around the emperor's neck which would not tighten. Meanwhile some of the young girls involved began to become panic and one ran to the empress. The plot was exposed and all of the girls involved underwent execution by the slow slicing method and their families were killed.

After the assassination attempt in 1542, Jiajing began to pay excessive attention to his Taoist pursuits while ignoring his imperial duties.

1.2 The Introduction for the Tourists Interested in Chinese Culture

Today we are going to Wudang Mountain. It covers an area of 312 square kilometers. In 1994, the monasteries and buildings were made a UNESCO World Cultural Heritage Site. Let's see the comments made by the experts. Kaosia, the expert of UNESCO, said, "Mt. Wudang area is certainly one of the most beautiful areas in the world because it combines ancient wisdom, historic architecture and natural beauty." Sumimtardia, the expert of UNESCO, said, "the great past of China is still solid in Mountain Wudang." Yang Tingbao (杨廷保), vice-chairman of the World Architect Association, said that "the paradise in the world occupied a more prominent position than the other five national famed mountains."

The mountain is located within the same latitude—around the 30 degrees north latitude—as many other mystical places, such as Bermuda Triangle, Egypt's Great Pyramids, and Mount Everest, the highest peak and the lowest bottom in the world. Some famous rivers, such as the Nile of Egypt, the Changjiang River of China and the Mississippi of America, all flow into the sea in the latitude. Besides, many spectacular geological wonders can be found in the latitude; only in China, we have the tide of Qiantang River, Huangshan Mountain of Anhui Province, Lushan Mountain of Jiangxi Province and Emei Mountain of Sichuan Province. Interestingly, most of high-quality tea leaves are also produced in the latitude, so don't forget to taste the tea here.

Do you know which emperor is enshrined on Wudang Mountain? Emperor Zhenwu, a tortoise-snake figure. In the spring of 1994, a photo of the mountain was taken from the sky. Can you imagine what it looks like? The whole mountain looks as if a snake is inter-twisting a tortoise. Is it a wonder?

What made Wudang Mountain so popular? At that time, the political centers of China were Chang'an (present Xi'an), Kaifeng and Luoyang. It's 280 kilometers from Xi'an, 290 kilometers from Luoyang and 400 kilometers from Kaifeng. It's neither too far nor too near to the political centers, which is good for the development of Taoism. On the other hand, the height of the mountain is suitable for pilgrims to hike up; the hike can be done, however, it is not easy.

More than two thousand years ago, Yinxi, the commissioner of Hanguguan Pass（函谷关）, was the first recorded person to come to Wudang Mountain. He had a meeting with the philosopher Lao Tzu. Yinxi implored Lao Tzu to set his thoughts down in writing. The book was *Tao Te Ching*, which would be viewed as the philosophical basis of Taoism later. "Tao" means "way"; it implies the essential, unnamable process of the universe. "Te" means "virtue" in the sense of "personal character", "inner strength" or "integrity". "Ching" means "canon", "great book", or "classic". *Tao Te Ching* is the second most published and translated book in history, only behind the *Bible*. As for Yinxi, he was so inspired by *Tao Te Ching* that he turned his back on his former life, and set off in search of somewhere to practice Lao Tzu's philosophy. The place he eventually chose was Wudang Mountain.

As we know, Wudang Mountain is a holy land of Taoism. But do you know many Buddhist monks lived here before the Tang Dynasty (618-907)? In the Tang Dynasty, Tang Emperors claimed themselves to be the descendants of Lao Tzu, which is beneficial to the development of Taoism. During the Tang Dynasty (618-907), Yao Jian（姚简）, an official, prayed for rain at Wudang Mountain and succeeded; the first site of worship—the Five Dragon Temple—was constructed. But in 761, a Buddhist monk, Huizhong（慧忠）from Wudang Mountain gave a sermon in Chang'an and was appreciated by Emperor Suzong（唐肃宗）and Daizong（唐代宗）and respected as a national master. Four Buddhist temples（太乙、延昌、香严、长寿）were built and Buddhism overwhelmed Taoism at Wudang Mountain.

Do you know the Five Elements? They are wood, fire, earth, metal, and water. According to the theory, the five elements damaged and succeeded one another in a cyclic process governed by the cosmic principles of Yin (Earth, female, passive, absorbing) and Yang (Heaven, male, active, penetrating), giving rise to all of nature, the seasons and different dynasties. Song Dynasty belongs to the element of fire, so the god of fire was worshiped. In order to balance Yin and Yang, the god of water was also worshiped. One night, Emperor Huizong of the Song Dynasty（宋徽宗，1119-1125）had a dream about the god of fire. A Taoist interpreted the dream that a palace should be built in the south for the god of water, for the south was in the charge of the god of fire; only the god of water could conquer the god of fire. In this way, he could free himself from troubles. The place Emperor Huizong chose to build the palace was Wudang Mountain; this was the first time Taoism outweighed Buddhism in this area.

In the Yuan Dynasty, Qiu Chuji（丘处机），a Taoist monk, advocated Buddhism, Confucianism and Taoism should be synergetic. He absorbed the filial piety from Confucianism and moral discipline from Buddhism; Taoism enjoyed great popularity in different social circles. Genghis khan（成吉思汗）sent for him and appreciated his ability. Emperor Renzong of the Yuan Dynasty（元仁宗）happened to be born on March 3rd, the same birthday as Emperor Zhenwu, the main god enshrined on Wudang Mountain. As a result, Wudang Mountain received more attention from the government. During his reign, Zhang Shouqing（张守清）was ordered to pray for rain three times and succeeded each time.

In the 15th century, it reached its peak. Why? Let me tell you the reason. In 1399, Zhu Di, the fourth son of Zhu Yuanzhang (the first emperor of the Ming Dynasty), raised a rebellion and forced Emperor Jianwen（建文帝）—his nephew to vacate the throne. After Zhu Di seized the throne, he knew what he had done violated the feudal ethical code and the ministers might refuse to accept his ruling. So

Zhu Di tried to find an excuse to make his enthronement lawful. He declared that his power was granted by Emperor Zhenwu. Not long after he became emperor, he ordered some officials to oversee the construction of a large scale architectural complex on Wudang Mountain to show his gratitude to Emperor Zhenwu. It was said that many craftsmen were forced to carve the statue of Emperor Zhenwu. They racked their brains to do that task, but still Emperor Zhu Di was not satisfied with the imaginary man. At last, one of them found a way out; he created Emperor Zhenwu according to Zhu Di's look. In the 15th century, Wudang Mountain became the center of China Taoism.

Wudang Mountain is famous for its prefect combination of the natural and cultural scenery. The landscape, ancient architectural complex, Taoism culture and Wudang wushu appeal to people from home and abroad.

1.3 The Introduction for the Tourists from Beijing

I was told that you came from Beijing. Have you been to the Forbidden City in Beijing? Do you know there is a Forbidden Wall on Wudang Mountain? Is there any connection between the Forbidden City in Beijing and the Forbidden Wall on Wudang Mountain? There is some connection between the Forbidden City in Beijing and the Forbidden Wall on Wudang Mountain.

Both of them were commissioned by Zhu Di, the Yongle Emperor. Why did he do that? Let me tell you the story. Zhu Di, the Prince of Yan (the present Beijing), was very successful against the

Mongols. But Zhu Di was not the eldest son, so his father named Zhu Biao, his eldest brother, as crown prince. However, Zhu Biao died at the age of 38—before his father died. As a result, Zhu Biao's son Zhu Yunwen became emperor.

Zhu Yunwen regarded Zhu Di as his opponent; he was afraid that Zhu Di would seize his place one day. When Zhu Di traveled with his guards to pay tribute to his father, Zhu Yunwen took his actions as a threat and sent troops to repel him. Zhu Di was forced to leave in humiliation. In this case, Zhu Di raised a rebellion against Zhu Yunwen and succeeded. After coming to the throne, Zhu Di moved the capital from Nanjing to Beijing, and constructed the Forbidden City in Beijing. He knew what he had done violated the feudal ethical code, so he was also afraid that the ministers might refuse to accept his ruling. Zhu Di tried to find an excuse to make his enthronement lawful. He declared that his power was granted by Emperor Zhenwu. Not long after he became emperor, he commissioned a large scale construction on Wudang Mountain to show his gratitude to Emperor Zhenwu. He ordered to build the Forbidden Wall on Wudang Mountain.

1.4 The Introduction for the Tourists Whose Stay is during Rainy Days

I should be grateful to you because you bring us good luck. You may feel puzzled. Before your coming, we surfed the Internet and found that it would rain for three days. Do you know who is enshrined on Wudang Mountain? The answer is the god of water. Let me tell you the story:

One night, Emperor Huizong of the Song Dynasty (1119-1125) had a dream about the god of fire. A Taoist interpreted the dream that a palace should be built in the south for the god of water, for the south was in the charge of the god of fire; only the god of water could conquer the god of fire. In this way, he could separate himself from troubles. Emperor Huizong chose Wudang Mountain to build the palace.

Another wonder is that Wudang Mountain looks like a flame from a distance; on its top is the god of water. The god of water is Emperor Zhenwu, therefore comes the saying "Fei Zhen Wu Bu Zu Dang Zhi" which means that only Zhenwu enjoys the power and privilege to live here. Zhenwu is the most important god worshiped on Wudang Mountain. Seen from the sky, Wudang Mountain looks like a tortoise-snake figure，which happens to represent the god of water.

One of the earliest buildings—the Five Dragon Temple—was also constructed because of water. According to the *Annals of Wudang Mountain*, at the beginning of the 7th century, there was a serious drought, so the emperor Li Shimin（李世民）ordered Yaojian, the official of Junzhou to pray for rain. Yaojian succeeded and dispelled the drought, so the emperor issued an imperial edict to build Taoism temples. From then on, a lot of temples were ordered to be built at Wudang Mountain by royal families.

Water is mentioned twice in *Tao Te Ching*. In Chapter 8, "The supreme good is like water, nourishing all things. It is content with the low places that people disdain. Thus it is like the Tao." (上善若水。水善利万物而不争，处众人之所恶，故几于道。) In Chapter 78, "Nothing in the world is as soft and yielding as water. Yet for dissolving the hard and inflexible, nothing can surpass it. The soft overcomes the hard; the gentle overcomes the rigid. Everyone knows this is true, but few can put it into practice." (天下莫柔弱于水。而攻坚强者，莫之能胜。以其无以易之。弱之胜强。柔之胜刚。天下莫不知莫能行。) The water, which takes the form of the objects it touches in its course, provides a valuable model for Taoist conduct. The Taoist adept has created a similar model of human behavior which may be formulated as follows: Under all circumstances, one should behave like water, one should adjust to the requirements of the outer reality, and adapt himself or herself to all circumstances.

Do you know how many times water is addressed in the *Bible*? 626 times. Water equates to life being essential for drinking, cooking, even cleaning. Water can also be used symbolically. (1) Water may symbolize emotions or psychic energy. It is therefore important to notice whether the water is free flowing or stagnant, clean or foul. (2) Water is a common symbol for fertility, growth, creative potential (especially it takes the form of a reservoir or still lake), new life, or healing. (3) It is also a symbol for the unconscious. Deep water, oceans, seas, large lakes often symbolize the collective unconscious. Smaller bodies of water may symbolize the personal unconscious. (4) It is a feminine symbol, representing either your own femininity (whether you are a male or female), or your mother. It is therefore important to note your reaction to water in your dream. Are you afraid of water in real life? This may mean you are afraid of women (if you are a man), of your mother, or of your unconscious (hidden aspects that can be emotionally disturbing when brought to consciousness).

Extended Reading 2: Emperor Zhenwu

Zhenwu is one of the most influential gods in Taoism. In China, Zhenwu has more temples than any other gods. In Taoism, he was just a common god at the beginning. Because of the Emperor's devotion to Xuanwu in the 12th and 13th centuries, his status was raised quickly. In the 15th, 16th and 17th centuries (1368-1644), belief in him reached its peak. The government built large-scale temples on Wudang Mountain. Later, the common people also worshipped him.

Ancient Chinese observed the sky and divided the stars into four groups, and then imagined them as four animals, which were a bird, a tiger, a dragon and a figure combining a tortoise and a snake. As both the tortoise and the snake are regarded as lucky animals, they have long been worshiped by people. In the 12th century (in the Song Dynasty), the tortoise-snake figure was personified as Xuanwu and received greater respect.

What's the relationship between Xuanwu and Zhenwu? In ancient China, there were three kinds of naming taboo: 1) The naming taboo of the state（国讳）discouraged the use of the emperor's given name and those of his ancestors. For example, during the Qin Dynasty, Qin Shi Huang's given name Zheng（政）was avoided, and the first month of the year "Zheng Yue"（政月：the administrative month） was rewritten into "Zheng Yue"（正月：the upright month） and furthermore renamed as "Duan Yue"（端月：the proper/upright month）. 2) The naming taboo of the clan（家讳）discouraged the use of the names of one's own ancestors. 3) The naming taboo of the holinesses（圣人讳）discouraged the use of the names of respected people. For example, writing Confucius' name was taboo during the Jin Dynasty. There were three ways to avoid using a taboo character: 1) Leaving the character as a blank. For example, Guanshiyin was renamed as Guanyin in order to avoid the name of the Tang Emperor Li Shimin（李世民）. 2) Omitting a stroke in the character, especially the final stroke. 3) Changing the character to another one which usually was a synonym or sounded like the character being avoided. Xuanwu was renamed as Zhenwu in order to avoid the name of Zhao Xuanlang（赵玄郎）, who was respected as an ancestor by the Song emperors.

1.5 At the Mountain Gate

Now we can see a stone gate. The construction of which started in 1988 and ended in 1990. It is 11.9 meters high and 21.6 meters wide. With a mortise-and-tenon structure, it is made up of 136 parts.

The three characters "Wu Dang Shan" are copies of Mu Xin's handwriting. Mu Xin, one of Emperor Zhu Di's sons-in-law, was a famous poet and calligrapher. Do you know his story? He married Zhu Di's daughter, Princess Changning（常宁公主）, who died at the age of 22. He was worried that he was to blame for his wife's death.

In order to show his loyalty, he volunteered to be in charge of the construction of the palaces and temples at Wudang Mountain.

Now we are in the Tourists' Center. This center was put in use in July, 2006. Taizipo Palace (Crown Prince Palace) is a transfer center and a necessary road to each scenic spot. It's 11 kilometers away from the Tourists' Center and takes us about 20 minutes to go there. In the Transfer Center, those who want to take a cable car to the Golden Hall can take another sightseeing bus to the Qiongtai Temple, and those who want to hike up to the Golden Hall can take another bus to Wuyaling（乌鸦岭）. Along the road, we can also visit Taizipo Palace, Zixiao Palace, Xiaoyaogu Valley and Nanyan Palace.

There are many windings here, so if you feel bus-sick, please let me know and we can offer you some plastic bags free of charge.

II. Taizipo Scenic Zone

2.1 Needle-Rubbing Well

All the temples and palaces on Wudang Mountain were built according to the myth about Zhenwu. Zhenwu, Crown Prince of State Jingle, refined himself in Taizipo Palace (Crown Prince Palace) at the age of 15. After 12 years, he achieved nothing, so he was totally depressed and decided to give up; however, when he came here, he met God Ziqi, in the form of an old woman, rubbing an iron pestle in order to get a needle. But Zhenwu could not understand the deep meaning at that time, so he continued his journey. When he came to Huixin Convent (回心庵), he suddenly realized that "Perseverance will prevail", so he came back to continue his refinement and finally he flew to Heaven in Nanyan Palace. He won honorary title in the Qiongtai Temple and the highest-level architectural style of the Golden Hall shows how respectful and powerful he was in the country.

The Needle-Rubbing Well is located in a high position with an area of 1,543 square meters. It was initially built during the reign of Emperor Kangxi (1662-1722), and rebuilt in 1852 and in 1981.

The Needle-Rubbing Well is also called Chunyang Temple (纯阳

宫，Pure Sunshine Temple). How did the temple get its name? According to Wudang Taoism, it is this place that receives the first beam of sunshine. Another version is that Lu Dongbin, with the title of Chunyangzi（纯阳子）, was worshiped here.

The main building is the Master Hall（祖师殿）, which was donated by Zhifu official（知府，similar to present governor of a province）. On the top of the temple, we can see two boys. It was said they were sons of Jiang Ziya（姜子牙）. Inside the temple, we can see the statues of young Zhenwu, Lu Dongbin, Zhenwu's parents and Chen Tuan. Above the middle shrine, we can see four Chinese characters "Bao He Tai He（保合太和）", which mean that Wudang Mountain, where Yin and Yang are balanced, is a favorable place for things to grow. There is another stele: Jun Ji Yu Tian（峻极于天）, which mean that people should be wise enough to the realize the existence of the Tao in the universe and follow the natural laws. On the walls are eight fresco paintings, made in 1862. They present the whole legend of Zhenwu from his birth to his refinement at the mountain and then to his being a god. The first one tells us that Zhenwu left the court; the second one tells that Zhenwu came to Wudang Mountain; the third one tells that Zhenwu separated himself from the soldiers who were sent to follow him to Wudang Mountain by his parents; the fourth one tells that monkeys sent him fruits while Zhenwu refined himself here; the fifth one tells a crow led Zhenwu and a black tiger made a path for Zhenwu; the sixth one tells Zhenwu beat demons; the seventh one tells Zhenwu's master gave Zhenwu a test; the last one tells Zhenwu flew to Heaven and traveled around the heavenly and earthly world.

This is Lao Mu Pavilion. This is the statue of Lao Mu. Look! She is holding an iron pestle with her head leaned to one side. It seems that she is enlightening Zhenwu who wants to give it up.

Here we can see some sea animal fossils. The animals lived about 450 million years ago, which indicates this place was once a sea.

2.2 Introduction

This is a parking lot. We can see Fuzhen Bridge. It's 16 meters long and was built in 1416.

Now we have reached a platform. Looking back, we can see no steps. It means that we have to make every effort to succeed. When we make it, we will feel proud and satisfied. But after the short break, we have to move towards the next target.

Here we can see three big Chinese characters "Tai Zi Po", written by Mu Xin, one of Emperor Yongle's sons-in-law. "Tai Zi" means crown prince. It is said that the Crown Prince in State Jingle refined himself in this place at the very beginning. Why is it called "Po"? "Po" means slope, because the palace stands on a slope at a 60-degree angle. It is also named as Fuzhen Palace (复真观). "Fuzhen" means coming back to refine himself again. Let me tell you the myth. After several decades, he had achieved nothing, so he was totally depressed and decided to give it up; however, when he came here, he met his master, God Ziqi, in the form of an old woman, grinding an iron pestle on a stone by a well. He was surprised and asked: "Granny, what are you grinding a pestle for?" She replied without raising her head, "To make a needle." Astonished, Zhenwu asked, "The pestle is so thick and a needle is so tiny, so when can you finish your task?" She smiled and answered, "To grind a pestle into a needle, you have to make every effort to achieve the goal." Suddenly, Zhenwu realized that it was his lack of persistence that had led to his failure. After saying goodbye to the old woman, he returned and continued to refine himself here.

Taizipo Palace (Crown Prince Palace) was initially built in 1412 and repaired three times during the reign of Emperor Kangxi. It covers an area of 1,600 square meters.

Four wonders here are "Four Gates within One Mile", "Nine Winding Yellow River Walls", "One Pillar and Twelve Girders" and "Sweet Bay Laurel".

Four Gates within One Mile: This is the first of the four famous gates within one mile. Here, we can see four gates. Most Chinese people today will go through the four periods of education: primary school, junior high school, senior high school and university. It's also "four gates". It remains unclear whether it is a coincidence or a profound theory implied in the ancient buildings here.

2.3 Nine Winding Yellow River Walls

Now we can see 71-meter long red-jacketed walls. They are 1.5 meters thick and 2.5 meters high. They are named as Nine Winding Yellow River Walls.

Different people have different views about the origin of the name "Nine Winding Yellow River Walls". In China, nine has special meanings. Do you know them? In ancient times, the heaven was divided into nine layers. So Jiu Tian（九天，the ninth layers of the Heaven）refers to the highest place. Oppositely, Jiu Quan（九泉）refers to the lowest place, where the dead lives. Jiu Zhou（九州，nine provinces）refers to the whole China. Great Yu（大禹，2200 BC-2100 BC）was a legendary ruler famed for his introduction of flood control. After taming the floods, Yu was familiar with all regions of what was then Han Chinese territory, and then he divided the Chinese "world" into nine provinces and collected bronze in tribute from each one. Then, he cast the metal into nine large tripod cauldrons representing the nine provinces. It was he who received the tributes of bronze from the nine provinces, so Jiu Ding（九鼎，Nine Tripod Cauldrons）refers to the highest authority. Because ancient Chinese revered the number nine, the emperor was considered the "nine five supremacy" （九五之尊）in the *Book of Change*（《易经》）; the palaces, which are nine bays wide and five bays deep, are exclusively for emperors.

Taoist monks believe that people who donate to the palaces or temples will be protected by gods; the donations include clothing, scriptures（经书）, josses（造像）, buildings, ritual instruments（法器）, candle lamps, bells, vegetarian food, and yellow paper money for worshiping the gods（香表）, called "nine kinds of charitable and pious deeds". Some people say Qian Kun means Heaven and Earth; those representing Heaven are usually named with nine in Taoism (In Taoism, three means stable, six means smooth and nine means sacred). In fact, the direct route to the main hall is very short. Why did people build such a winding route? Their purpose was to make the palace mysterious and imposing. Therefore, Nine Winding Yellow River Walls reflect not only the thoughts of Taoism but also the style of imperial building.

2.4 The Courtyard before the Dragon-Tiger Hall

Now we have entered the second gate, opposite it is the third one. Pass the third gate, turn left and we can see the fourth gate. In the Ming Dynasty, this is the only access to the Golden Hall.

This is a brick-made incense burner. It is the best preserved, but now pilgrims are not allowed to burn incense here in order to protect it.

In the middle is a screen wall. It aims to protect people from falling into the cliff and prevent the demons from entering the hall. On the screen wall, there are three Chinese characters "Fu, Lu and Shou", which mean luckiness, prosperity and longevity respectively. After burning the incense, pilgrims would turn three times counterclockwise and walk forwards to touch the characters. If they touch Fu, it means they will be lucky; Lu, it means they will be rich; Shou, it means they will live longer. Then they would go to the platform to hit the clock, which had been moved to Hubei Provincial Museum, in the hope that Emperor Zhenwu could hear their prayer. On fine days, the Golden Hall can be seen here.

Can you see some stakes? Do you know their functions? Horses used to be tied to them. This was once a place for pilgrims to have a rest.

Here we can see two tablets made in 1690. The one on the back of a turtle records the geological importance of Taizipo Palace and what it had suffered and how people donated money to rebuild the place. The other one tells us the names of the donators, but we can not see it clearly because it had been weathered and eroded.

2.5 Dragon-Tiger Hall

Dragon-Tiger Hall is the entrance to the main hall. There is a Dragon-Tiger Hall in every important palace on Wudang Mountain. We can see four Chinese characters "Ti Hui Chang Chun"（体慧长春）on the horizontal board. "Ti" means the origin of the world, "Hui" means wisdom. It means Xuanwu has infinite wisdom and his thoughts and spirit will last forever.

On the left is the statue of General Dragon in charge of the officials and promotion. On the right is the statue of General Tiger in charge of the dead, the sick, and the aged. The powerful white tiger is molded very kind, and the tame dragon has ferocious expressions. This shows Taoists' belief: positive and negative elements should be balanced.

Can you see a well? It is called "Tear-Dripping Well". When Zhenwu came to Wudang Mountain at the age of 15, his mother was loath to part with her son; she followed him here and cried sadly. A pool formed from her tears. Do you know how deep the well is? It is as deep as mother's love.

In the eastern room are some pictures of Wudang Mountain in different seasons and in the western room are the exhibits showing how Taoist monks stay healthy.

2.6 The Main Hall (Fuzhen Hall)

The Main Hall is the main part of the palace. In 1412 (the tenth year of Emperor Yongle of the Ming Dynasty), Fuzhen Hall was built and expanded during the reign of Emperor Jiajing. However, at the end of the Ming Dynasty it was largely damaged. Then, in 1686 (the 25th year of Emperor Kangxi of the Qing Dynasty), local officials and pious believers donated some money to repair it. Since it was difficult to regain the royal grandeur of the past, many folk practices of building construction were also used in the reconstruction of the Main Hall. So viewing the hall today one can see the coexistence of both royal and folk building styles as well as the combination of the architectural skills and arts of the Ming and Qing Dynasties.

We can see four Chinese characters "Yun Yan Chu Bu" （云岩初步）. "Yun Yan" means Zhenwu refined himself in a difficult situation and "Chu Bu" means it was the first place for Zhenwu to refine himself. There is a couplet: 五百羽林仪杖分列铁骑鸣处震威远，三千世界名山独峙炉烟霭时流祚多. It means that the 500 soldiers who followed Emperor Zhenwu to Wudang Mountain are brave enough to stamp out the demons in the world, so they enjoy great popularity everywhere. Wudang Mountain is so famous in the world that many pilgrims come here to burn incense hoping the rising smoke can bring them happiness and good luck. Another couplet: 复见天心虚危应宿峰峰碧，真成神武旗剑扬烟处处玄. It means that there are so many people who believe in Emperor Zhenwu that the shrines for Emperor Zhenwu can be found here and there on Wudang

Mountain.

In this hall, the statues of Zhenwu are the biggest colored wooden sculptures. By now, it has existed for 600 years. We can also see the statues of Golden Boy and Jade Girl, the attendants of Emperor Zhenwu. Now, Golden Boy and Jade Girl mean the perfect couple in the field of entertainment.

Above the statue, we can see "灵光普照", which means that if we are loyal, pious and honest, Emperor Zhenwu will bless us.

Inside the hall, we can see the couplet: 赤脚常怀赤心爱民如保赤子，青衿每放青眼恩德堪配青天, which means that Emperor Zhenwu takes care of people as babies; the intellectuals are so respectful to Emperor Zhenwu that they think he can be compared to Heaven, which brings them everything that they need to survive.

2.7 Crown Prince Study Hall

Crown Prince Study Hall was built on the highest position of the palace in the 14th century. The hall is regarded as the only place on Wudang Mountain for people to pray for good luck in their learning.

It is said that Zhang Shixun（张士逊）, Prime Minister of the Northern Song Dynasty, once came here with his mother to ask for Emperor Zhenwu's favor and protection as a child. Luckily, he passed the imperial examination and was promoted to Prime Minister. From then on, those hoping their children to succeed in learning and life often come here to pray for their children.

2.8 Scripture Hall

Scripture Hall is the place for Taoist monks to read the scriptures and to worship the deities. Every morning and evening, Taoists gather to read scriptures and to worship the deities. In every important palace of Wudang Mountain there is a scripture hall. This Scripture Hall was built in the 14th century and renovated in the 17th century, so it has many architectural crafts of the two dynasties (the Ming and Qing Dynasties) and a lot of historical and research value.

On the shrine of the Scripture Hall is the statue of the god of vanquishing evils（荡魔天尊）, another image of Zhenwu. It means that common people hope Emperor Zhenwu can stamp out all the demons and punish the evildoers.

Can you see a tree in front of the Scripture Hall? What do you call it? Bay laurel, sweet bay, bay tree, true laurel, laurel tree, or simply laurel? Can you guess its age? It is about 400 years old. Every October, the flowers give off fragrance that can be smelt several hundred miles away.

In China, the tree has a rich connotation. It has been a sign of good luck in imperial examinations, the highest level of academic competition under the feudal system dating back to the Sui Dynasty (6th century). Why? The sweet-scented tree blossoms in August, when imperial examinations were held.

There is a story: In Jiangxi Province in the 13th century, there was a flourishing laurel which covered a large area in a yard. Unfortunately, it was reduced to a naked trunk in a war fire. In spring a few years later, new shoots popped out from the trunk's base and the person living in the yard succeeded in the imperial examination. Since then, people have been connecting the tree with good luck. If a Chinese congratulates a person who succeeds in an exam or a competition, he will say that he has picked a laurel branch.

It has also been a symbol of noble virtues. Usually, plants bloom in spring, but laurel trees blossom in cold autumn. They add beauty to the season; poets and intellectuals always regard that a laurel tree distinguishes itself from others.

Extended Reading 3: Laurel Tree

Laurel tree, also known as sweet bay, bay tree, true laurel, bay laurel, or simply laurel, was used to fashion the laurel wreath of ancient Greece, a symbol of the highest status. The Greeks gave a wreath of laurels to the victors in the Pythian Games because the games were in honor of Apollo, and the laurel was one of his symbols, but the victor in the Olympic Games had a wreath of wild olives. How does the custom come into being? Let me tell you a Greek legend.

Apollo, the god of the sun, insulted Cupid for playing with bow and arrows. Apollo was a great warrior and said to him, "What have you to do with warlike weapons, saucy boy? Leave them for hands worthy of them."

Cupid was offended and took two arrows, one of gold and one of lead. The gold one was supposed to incite love, while the lead one was supposed to incite hatred. With the leaden shaft, Cupid shot the nymph Daphne and with the golden one, he shot Apollo through the heart. Apollo loved Daphne, and she in turn hated him. In fact, she rejected her many potential lovers. His father warned her saying, "Your own face will forbid it." By saying this he meant that she was too beautiful to keep all her potential lovers away forever. However, she begged her father to let her remain unmarried.

Apollo continually followed her, begging her to stay, but the nymph continued her flight. Seeing that Apollo was bound to catch her, she called upon her father, "Help me! Open the earth to enclose me, or change my form, which has brought me into this danger!"

Suddenly, her skin turned into bark, her hair became leaves, and her arms were transformed into branches. She stopped running as her feet became rooted to the ground. Since Apollo could no longer take her as his wife, he vowed to tend her as his tree, and promised that her leaves would decorate the heads of leaders as crowns. Apollo also used his powers of eternal youth and immortality to render her ever green. Since then, the leaves of the bay laurel tree have never known decay.

There are also some phrases such as "to rest on one's laurels", which means "to be satisfied with the degree of success one has already achieved and to refrain from further effort." For the sake of completeness, "to look to one's laurels" means "to be on one's guard against rivals; to endeavor to maintain one's lead in a field in which one has already excelled."

In Chinese folklore, there is a great laurel tree on the moon, and the Chinese name for the laurel （月桂）, literally is translated to "moon-laurel". Wu Gang was a man who aspired to immortality, but he could not concentrate on it. When the deities discovered this, they sentenced Wu Gang to fell the laurel tree; however, since the laurel regenerated immediately when cut, it could never be felled. The phrase "Wu Gang chops the tree"（吴刚伐木）is sometimes used to refer to endless toil (Adapted from http://baike.baidu. com/view/8810. htm).

2.9 The Screen Wall with a Chinese Character "Fu"

Wudang Mountain is not only a world cultural heritage site, but also a revolutionary base. Here we can see a screen wall with a Chinese character "Fu"（福）. It was written in 1931 by He Long, a revolutionist. Behind it are the Chinese characters "Shi Xing Tu Di Ge Ming"（实行土地革命）. It means to carry out the land reform, which was between 1927 and 1937.

2.10 Five-Story Building

Five-Story Building, stilt houses, 15.8 meters high, is the tallest existing wooden building on Wudang Mountain. It was built completely according to the shape of the mountain, with no excavating, because it tried to achieve the harmony between man and nature.

Five-Story Building is famous for one pillar and twelve girders. The pillar and overlapped and carefully arranged girders support the whole building. This architectural framework was the masterpiece of ancient wooden buildings and has received praise from many people, among whom is Li Ruihuan, a national leader, who came here in 1994.

The building takes the shape of stilt houses. It can also be found in folk residence. It is usually built in steep mountain areas. In China, it is popular especially among the ethnic groups, such as Tujia, Miao, Zhuang, Yao, Dong, etc. Do you know the advantages of the stilt houses? The design makes use of land that might be otherwise unsuitable for housing. The elevation serves to keep out vermin and offers protection from animals. The space beneath the house may be used for storage. They are really ecologically friendly homes. As far as I know, the stilt houses can also be built beside rivers, especially in places prone to flooding. In Indonesia, Singapore, and other countries, "kelong" are built for fishing, but may double as offshore housing. Stilt houses are also gaining popularity in the United States, particularly along the Gulf Coast, where the threat of hurricanes is severe.

2.11 Xiaoyaogu Valley

Now we have arrived at Xiaoyaogu Valley. This is called "Sword River Bridge". Zhang Shouqing and his disciples raised some money and built it in 1324. Expanded in 1412, it was the biggest of the 46 bridges on Wudang Mountain in the Ming Dynasty, also the earliest stone bridge in the western part of Hubei Province. There is a myth about the bridge. When Zhenwu came to Wudang Mountain at the age of 15, his mother was loath to part with his son. She followed him here and pulled him back by the hem of his clothes. Determined to refine himself here, Zhenwu took out his sword and cut the hem off and the mountain into two halves. A river came into being; mother and son were separated.

There are two Kungfu shows every day. One is at 10:30 am and the other is at 3:30 pm.

Look at the thatched house. In 2008, *Heaven Sword And Dragon Sabre* was shot here and in 2009, *Karate Kid* was also shot here.

Can you see some monkeys now? Attempts to attract monkeys had been made three times, but resulted in failure. In 2002, the government invested more than 0.2 million yuan and employed six persons to do the task. Eight months later, they familiarized themselves with the food habits of the monkeys. There is a large food variability in summer and fall; the staple foods were woody leaves, flowers, seeds and fruits. But in winter and spring, food availability is poor, so the employers spread peanuts and corn around the valley. In this way, the number of the monkeys has increased to more than 200.

Do you know the meaning of the two characters "Xiao Yao"? They mean "carefree". "Xiao Yao You" is an article written by Zhuangzi (396 BC-289 BC), one of the two defining figures (Zhuangzi and Lao Tzu) of Chinese Taoism. Zhuangzi and Lao Tzu were jointly called "Laozhuang" by later generations. He was a firm believer in inaction, promoting the free realm and the harmony between nature and man. Throughout history, his teachings have been particularly favored by Chinese scholars and artists, many of whom have been inspired by Zhuangzi's philosophy.

Have you seen the film *Zhuangzi Tests His Wife*(《庄子试妻》), a

1913 Hong Kong drama film directed by Li Minwei（黎民伟）? It is the first ever feature film（故事片）in Hong Kong cinema. It also became the first ever Chinese film to be shown abroad, when it was exhibited in the Chinese communities of Los Angeles and San Francisco. In the film, philosopher Zhuangzi meets a woman fanning the newly built grave of her dead husband because she desires to marry again. On returning home, Zhuangzi decides to put his wife to the test by faking his own death. His wife is grief-stricken and goes into mourning. While funeral arrangements are in progress, a handsome young man comes to call on Zhuangzi. Later, there is a talk of marriage between Zhuangzi's wife and the man. However, the young man falls ill; his servant says that taking the brain of a living or a newly dead person is the only way to cure him. The story ends with Zhuangzi burying his wife after she commits suicide for being disloyal to her husband.

III. Zixiao Scenic Zone (Purple Heaven Palace)

3.1 Introduction

Zixiao Palace was first built at the beginning of the 12th century [during the reign of Emperor Huizong, Song Dynasty (1119-1125)]. One night, Emperor Huizong of the Song Dynasty had a dream about the god of fire. A Taoist interpreted the dream that a temple should be built in the south for the god of water, for the south is in the charge of the god of fire; only the god of water can conquer the god of fire. In this way, he could separate himself from troubles. Emperor Huizong chose Wudang Mountain to build the palace, however it was damaged in the 13th century [at the end of Song Dynasty (1127-1276)]. When Kublai（忽必烈）became the first emperor of the Yuan Dynasty, he publicized Taoism and started a large scale construction on Wudang Mountain in order to win the hearts and minds of the local people.

The palace has the best Fengshui. It sits at the foot of a mountain which blocks the wind and sand from the north, so it is the best preserved palace on Wudang Mountain. Besides, facing south, it can allow a lot of sunshine into the halls. Do you know the name of the peak? It is called Zhanqi Peak（展旗峰）. Zhan means fluttering, and qi means flag. The peak looks like the backboard of a chair. On the left is Green Dragon Peak and on the right is White Tiger Peak. These two peaks look like the armrests of a chair. Zixiao Palace looks like an emperor sitting on the chair. We can also see two round hills. They are called "Big Pearl Peak" (大宝珠峰) and "Small Pearl Peak" (小宝珠峰). They look like the fish eyes in the Taiji Eight Diagrams and the axis looks like the division in the diagrams. Because of the elegant surroundings and pleasant weather, the place is thought to be a blessed place.

Historically, Zixiao Palace was a place for royal families to pray, so it was carefully arranged and exquisitely furnished. Emperors of the Song, Yuan, Ming and Qing Dynasties often set up altars here to practice the worship of ancestors and pray for favorable weather, in the hope that the state would become prosperous and the people would live peacefully. Taoists believed the gods would protect them from disasters and prolong their lives. All the buildings in Zixiao Palace are arranged along the North-South axis. On the axis lie Dragon-Tiger Hall, Shifangtang Hall, the Grand Hall and the Parent Hall from the lower to the higher. The Grand Hall, the most important hall, sits on a three-layer platform, whose purpose is to prevent damage from moisture. Moreover, the height of the platform corresponds to the importance of the buildings. A high building adds strength, sophistication too and stateliness to large buildings. The design and arrangement of the palace reflect the solemn dignity of the royal court.

At present, the Taoism Association of Wudang Mountain is

located here. Because of its high status in Taoism, many important Taoism events are held here. Here we can see some Taoist monks. To respect Taoist monks, we call them "Dao Zhang"（道长） which means Masters. If we meet some elderly Taoist monks, we should not ask their ages, for it is a taboo in Taoism. Now we are going to enter the palace. Please remember not to step on the threshold. No photos inside the palace! No shouting!

3.2 Yujichi Pond

This is Yujichi Pond（禹迹池）. In 1982, three ritual instruments used in Taoist mass—a golden dragon, a jade circle and inscriptions （金龙、玉壁和山简） were found in the pond. Let me tell you the story. Zhu Bai（朱柏） was one of Emperor Zhu Yuanzhang's sons. Zhu Yuanzhang was the first emperor of the Ming Dynasty. During the reign of Zhu Yunwen （朱允炆）, the third emperor of the Ming Dynasty, he began to suppress feudal lords. Zhu Bai, his uncle, felt threatened, and came to Wudang Mountain with the three instruments during the Lantern Festival in 1399. It was believed that these instruments could be used to communicate with God. Zhu Bai buried these instruments on Wudang Mountain in hope that they could help him escape from the disasters. Unfortunately, three months later, under Emperor Zhu Yunwen's pressure, he burned himself in a fire. Zhu Yunwen's reign was short (1398-1402); these instruments were precious.

3.3 Golden Water Bridge

The winding brook before us is the Golden Water Bridge. How did it get its name? According to the theory of Five Elements, the west is associated with gold, so the water coming from the west is called "golden water". It functions both as decoration and fire control. In Beijing, there are also many other ones named Golden Water Bridge.

Extended Reading 4: Features of Taoism Architecture

1) Horizontal emphasis. Taoism architecture stresses the visual impact of the width of the buildings. This contrasts with Western church, which tends to grow in height and depth. The halls and palaces have rather low ceilings when compared to equivalent stately buildings in the West.

2) Bilateral symmetry. Another important feature is its emphasis on articulation and bilateral symmetry, which signifies balance.

3) Enclosure. Western architectural practices typically involve surrounding a building by an open yard. This contrasts with Taoism architecture, which involves constructing buildings or building complexes that take up an entire property but encloses open spaces within itself.

4) Hierarchical. The hierarchy and importance of buildings in Taoism architecture are based on the strict placement of buildings in a complex. Buildings with doors facing the front are considered more important than those facing the sides. Buildings facing away from the

front of the property are the least important. As well, buildings in the rear and more private parts of the property are held in higher esteem and reserve for elder members of the family.

5) Geomancy concepts. Concepts from Fengshui and mythic concepts of Taoism are usually present in the construction and layout of Chinese architecture, from common residences to imperial and religious structures. This includes the use of:

- Screen walls facing the main entrance of the house, which stems from the belief that evil things travel on straight lines.

- Talismans or images of door gods displayed on doorways to ward evil and encourage the flow of good fortune.

- Orienting the structure with its back to elevated landscape and ensuring that there is water in the front.

- Ponds, pools, wells, and other water sources are usually built into the structure, for water can be used to collect Qi.

Adapted from http://arts.cultural-china.com/en/83Arts4935.html

3.4 Dragon-Tiger Hall

There are Dragon-Tiger Halls in all the important palaces on Wudang Mountain, such as Zixiao Palace, Taizipo Palace and Nanyan Palace. On the left is the statue of General Dragon and on the right is the statue of General Tiger. The General Dragon has a ferocious expression and the White Tiger wears a pleasant expression. In Taoism, Dragon belongs to Yang, and Tiger belongs to Yin. So it reflects the idea that Yin and Yang should be balanced.

These two colorfully painted, gilded mud statues are very

precious; they were carved by Liu Yuan（刘元）, one of the most important artists in the Yuan Dynasty, whose works are rarely found now. On Wudang Mountain, a lot were built in the Yuan Dynasty, such as the stone hall (Tianyi Zhenqing Hall) and the Fate-Changing Hall. In the niche is a colorfully-painted statue of Wang Shan. He was the most important among the 500 guardian deities on Wudang Mountain. He has three eyes and holds a steel whip. He is worshiped only in Lingguan Hall（灵官殿）of the Palace of Supreme Harmony and the Dragon-Tiger Hall of Zixiao Palace.

3.5 Imperial Tablet Pavilion

This is an Imperial Tablet Pavilion. In each important palace，there are two Imperial Tablet Pavilions. One stele（《下大岳太和山道士》碑文）records Emperor Chengzhu's regulations to govern Wudang Mountain; the other（《御制大岳太和山道宫》碑文）records the reason why Emperor Yongle built the palaces and temples on Wudang Mountain and the process of the construction.

Imperial Tablet Pavilion, the symbol of important palaces, is a unique construction of the Ming Dynasty. According to the history, the carvings on the stele, deriving from the inscriptions on the tortoise, represent one of the important phases of inscriptions. Ancient people thought only huge tortoises enjoy the privilege of bringing imperial edicts to the common people.

3.6 Stone Lions

This is a pair of stone lions, symbolizing imperial power and dignity. Can anybody tell which is male and which is female? The one on the east playing with a ball is a male, and the ball is said to represent state unity. The other one is a female. Underneath one of its fore claws is a cub, a symbol of perpetual imperial succession. Look, father is always playing with football while mother is taking care of the baby. These two lions were sent by Taiwanese in 2005. They are different from the ones from the north, which don't lean their heads to one side.

In the Buddhist faith, the lion is considered as a divine animal of nobleness and dignity, which can protect the truth and keep off evils. In Chinese folk tales, the lion has become a symbol of bravery, power and good luck. For this reason the stone lions are popular among the people and are commonly seen in front of the gates of ordinary families' homes.

It was also popular to decorate bridges with sculpted-stone lions for the same reason. The best known is Marco Polo Bridge（卢沟桥）, built from 1189 to 1192. The stone lions on the posts of the bridge are the most famous. It is said there are 485 lions in all. A famous proverb says, "the lions on Marco Polo Bridge are uncountable."

3.7 Pilgrimage Hall

Now we have come to the Pilgrimage Hall. Let's look at the walls. The walls look like expanding arms, welcoming the visitors from home and abroad. The Ba（八）-shaped walls consist of three parts: the basic bottom named Xu Mi（须弥座）, the body of the walls and the tiles on the top of the walls. Xu Mi comes from India. It is used to put the statues of Buddha and Bodhisattva. The main body of the wall is inlaid with flowers and rare auspicious animals.

Do you know what the two masts are used for? When major Taoism events are held here, the two masts are used to lift the Taoist flags instead of the national flags.

Why was it called "Pilgrimage Hall"? It is said that during the Ming Dynasty (1368-1644) the common pilgrims were only allowed to worship Emperor Zhenwu in this hall, while the Main Hall of the palace was exclusively for royal families and the commissioners sent by emperors to pray and sacrifice. That is why this hall is called "Pilgrimage Hall". Since the Qing Dynasty, Taoism did not enjoy such a high status as in the Ming Dynasty; this hall was also called Shifangtang Hall (十方堂) because the hall provided boarding and lodging for Taoists from other places (Shifangtang means "different places"). In Taoism, if the hall admits new Taoists, it is called Zi Sun Cong Lin (子孙丛林); if the hall provides boarding and lodging for the visiting Taoists, it is called Shi Fang Cong Lin (十方丛林). Shifangtang Hall was built in the Ming Dynasty (1412). It is recorded that Wudang Mountain became the center of Taoism in the Ming Dynasty, and many Taoists came to Wudang Mountain, so Shifangtang Hall was set up in order to care for the Taoists from other places. Historically, there was a rule that the Taoist monks of Quanzhen School did not need to carry food or firewood with them no matter where they went, for they would be housed and fed free of charge by the local Taoist monks in Shifangtang Hall if their ways of walking, saluting, and talking could prove they were true Taoists.

Now we are inside the Shifangtang Hall. In the middle of the mural is Zhang Sanfeng. Zhang Sanfeng, born in Liaoning Province, came to Wudang Mountain at the age of 70. Some say he lived to be more than 160, some say he lived to be more than 200, so his age is a mystery. Do you know the meaning of his name? San Feng（三丰）means heaven and earth. [(In the eight trigrams, San（三）represents heaven, or qian（乾）. Feng（丰）represents earth, or kun（坤）.] Settling down at Wudang Mountain, he was inspired by watching a snake fight a bird. By incorporating his training with wushu, Taoist internal alchemy, and Qigong, Zhang Sanfeng created Nei Jia Quan (Internal Martial Arts), which was later called Tai Chi Quan or the Tai Ji Quan 13 Style. The Tai Ji Quan 13 style has formed the basis of Wudang Internal Martial Arts, often referred to as Taoist Kungfu.

This mural is about eight immortals, seven men and one lady. They are Han Zhongli, Zhang Guolao, Han Xiangzi, Tieguai Li, Cao Guojiu, Lv Dongbin, Lan Caihe and He Xiangu（汉钟离、张果老、韩湘子、铁拐李、曹国舅、吕洞宾、蓝采和和何仙姑）. Let me tell you the legend: *The Eight Immortals Crossing the Sea* tells that a god invites the eight immortals to take part in a party appreciating peonies. On the way back, the Dragon King of the East Sea stops them and both sides start a furious dispute. At last, the eight immortals take out their talismans. With the help of other deities, they succeed in crossing the sea. It now has become an idiom meaning that each individual displays his talents to the fullest. It says that the Eight Immortals separately represent male, female, the old, the young, the rich, the noble, the poor, and the humble Chinese. The talismans that they use, which are called "Hidden Eight Immortals", all have certain meanings. Zhang Guolao's drum can augur life. Lv Dongbin's sword can subdue the evil. Han Xiangzi's flute can cause growth. He Xiangu's Water Lily can cultivate people through meditation. Tieguai Li's gourd can help the needy and relieve the distressed. Han Zhongli's fan can bring the dead back to life. Cao Guojiu's jade board can purify the environment. Lan Caihe's basket of flowers can communicate with gods. The Eight Immortals are the gods who punish evildoers and encourage people to do good, help those in distress and aid those in peril.

Here we can see 24 pictures. These stories tell us we should be filial to our parents. Filial piety is considered the first virtue in Chinese culture. The character "Xiao"（孝）is a combination of the character "Lao" (old) above the character "Zi" (son), that is, an elder being carried by a son. Someone may wonder why the pictures illustrating the Confucian culture are displayed in a Taoist temple. In the history of Taoism, Wang Chongyang and Qiu Chuji integrated Confucianism, Buddhism and Taoism together and formed a new school, Quanzhen School. People may think a Buddhist or Taoist monk is not filial to his parents; he leaves or abandons their families, parents, wives, and children. In fact, he has to gain permission from his parents if he wants to be a monk. Filial piety is advocated in different rehigions, but may be understood differently. For example, Buddhist monks think that all males are fathers and all females are mothers while Taoist monks emphasize that they should be filial to their biological parents.

Is filial piety regarded as an important virtue in your culture? The *Bible* tells people to be filial not only to parents but also to God, but in ancient China, people were required to be filial to both their parents and the feudal monarch.

Outside Shifangtang Hall, we can see four Chinese characters "Cun Xin He Fu（存心荷福）", which mean that pilgrims always remember Zhenwu's kindness and it is Zhenwu that brings them happiness.

Extended Reading 5: Twenty-Four Stories of Filial Piety

As one of the cores of Chinese culture, "filiality" is not only the moral code for maintaining family relationships in Chinese society for thousands of years, but also the traditional virtue of Chinese Nation. A Yuan-dynasty writer Guo Jujing（郭居敬）compiled the stories of 24 filial exemplars in ancient times and finished the Stories of Filiality. Reviewing these stories will help us better show filial respect for the elderly.

1. Filial Piety That Moved the Heaven（孝感动天）: Shun was a legendary ancient emperor and one of the Five Emperors. According to legend, his father Gusou（鼓叟, literally the blind old-man）, stepmother and half brother Xiang（象）plotted to kill him for many times: They let Shun revamp the roof of granary and set fire under the barn, Shun jumped to escape with two bamboo hats（斗笠）in hand; they also let Shun dig a well, but Gusou and Xiang filled soil to the well while digging, Shun then dug an underground tunnel to escape. Afterwards, Shun didn't resent and was still humble to his father and

loved his younger brother. Emperor Yao heard that Shun was a filial son with the talents of dealing with political affairs, and married off his two daughters to Shun. Through years of observation and tests, Emperor Yao selected Shun as his successor. After Shun ascended to the throne as the Son of Heaven, he still called on his father respectfully, and granted the leud title to Xiang（封象为诸侯）.

2. Entertain the Parents with Performances（戏彩娱亲）: Lao Laizi（老莱子）was an anchorite in the Spring and Autumn Period. He did farming at the south side of Meng Mountain（蒙山）to avoid the chaos in that period. He held great filiality to his parents. He fed the parents with the most delicious food, and entertained them with drum-shaped rattle playing when he was in his 70s, wearing colored clothes just like a child. Once, when he was on his way to bring water to his parents, he tumbled. He thought the parents might be worried about him, he just cried on the floor like a child, which made the parents laugh.

3. Feeding Parents with Deer's Milk（鹿乳奉亲）: Tan Tzu（郯子）was a man in the Spring and Autumn Period. As his parents were very old and suffered from eye disease, they had to drink deer's milk for treatment. Tan Tzu wore a piece of deerskin and groped into the mountains; he sneaked into herds of deer and squeezed deer's milk to serve his parents. On one occasion when he was taking milk, he saw a hunter was going to shoot a muntjac deer, Tan Tzu lifted the deerskin and appeared in a hurry, and then he told this hunter about the facts of squeezing deer's milk to cure his parents' disease. The hunter respected his filial piety and donated deer's milk. Finally, the

hunter escorted him out of the mountains.

4. Carrying Rice for More Than a Hundred Li for Parents（百里负米）: Zhong You（仲由）was a man in the State of Lu（鲁国）during the Spring and Autumn Period. He was a favorite disciple of Confucius. At an early age, as his family was poor, he often took wild vegetables as food, but still he carried sacks of rice for more than a hundred li for his parents. After his parents died, he became a high-ranked official. While enjoying sumptuous feast, he often missed his parents and sighed, "Even if I am willing to go back to the times when I ate wild vegetables and carried rice for more than a hundred li to raise my parents, how could that be possible?"

5. Paining Heart with Mother's Bitten Fingers（啮指心痛）: Zeng Shen（曾参）was a man in the State of Lu during the Spring and Autumn Period. He was also a favorite disciple of Confucius. When he was young, he often went into the mountains to gather firewood because his family was very poor. One day, a guest visited his home and his mother became perplexed. She bit her fingers with teeth, and Zeng Shen suddenly felt a pain in his heart. He knew his mother was calling on himself, so he quickly returned home with firewood. He then knelt down in front of his mother and asked what had happened. His Mother said, "A guest came unexpectedly. So I hope you to come back by biting my own fingers." Then Zeng Shen met with the guest and treated him with courtesy.

6. Obedient to Mother with Flimsy Clothes（芦衣顺母）: Min Sun（闵损）was a man in the State of Lu during the Spring and Autumn Period. He was a disciple of Confucius. Min Sun's mother

died early. Later his father took another wife, who gave birth to two sons. The stepmother mistreated Min Sun: in winter, while his two younger brothers wore winter clothes made of cotton, Min Sun only wore "reed catkins-padded cotton clothes." After knowing that Min Sun had been mistreated, his father wanted to divorce his wife. Min Sun fell on his knees and begged his father to forgive his stepmother. He said, "If mother stays at home, only I myself have to endure cold. But if you divorce mother, all three children have to suffer from cold." His father was deeply moved and took Min Sun's advice. The stepmother heard of this, felt remorseful and owned up to her mistakes. Subsequently, she treated Min Sun as her own son.

7. Taste Decoctions of Medicinal Ingredients Personally（亲尝汤药）:Liu Heng（刘恒）, Emperor Wen of the Han Dynasty, was famous for being kind and pious and never failed to wait upon his mother. His mother was ill for three years on bed and he was often sleepless. He always tasted the decoctions of medicinal ingredients for his mother's safety before letting her drink. He reigned for 24 years and emphasized virtues, advocated etiquette and paid attention to the development of agriculture, which made the West Han Dynasty stable, population flourish and economy recover and develop. His reign and that of Emperor Jing of the Han Dynasty were reputed together as the "Peaceful Reigns of Emperors Wen and Jing"（文景之治）.

8. Leave Better Food for Mother（拾葚异器）:Cai Shun（蔡顺） was a man in Runan (today's Henan) of the Han Dynasty. His father died when he was young and he was very pious to his mother. He lived in the era of chaos and famine. He could not but pick mulberries

as food for himself and his mother. One day, he encountered the solders, who asked him, "Why do you put red mulberries and black mulberries into two baskets separately?" Cai Shun answered, "The black mulberries are for my mother and the red mulberries are for myself." The solders had compassion for his piety and gave him some rice and one cow in respect.

9. Sell Oneself for Burial of Father（卖身葬父）: According to legend, Dong Yong（董永）lived in the East Han Dynasty. His mother died when he was young and later his father also died. Dong Yong sold himself to a rich family as a slave so that he could afford a funeral for his father. One day, he met a lady, who loved him for his kindness and filial piety, so they got married. She wove a lot of cloth in one month and bought back Dong Yong's freedom. In fact, she was the youngest of the seven daughters of the Queen of Heaven（王母娘娘）. The love between them was forbidden; her mother had her snatched back to Heaven, breaking up the happy couple. Some places are named based on the legend, which has been passed down from generation to generation, for example, Xiaogan (literally moved by filial piety) in Hubei Province claims that Dong Yong was a resident. Adapted from http://www.chinese.cn/cul/en/article/2010-10/14/ content _181168.htm

3.8 60-Year-Cycle Hall

Here you can have a rough idea of your fortune. The ancient astronomers divided zodiac into 12 equal segments, each of which has its own name and symbol. The purpose is to calculate the influence of the planets, especially on someone's life. Each year is associated with a different animal, as in "the year of the dog." According to one legend, in the sixth century BC Buddha invited all the animals in creation to come to him, but only twelve showed up: the Rat, Ox, Tiger, Rabbit, Dragon, Snake, Horse, Sheep, Monkey, Rooster, Dog, and Pig. Buddha rewarded each animal with a year bearing its personality traits. Legend describes the order of the zodiac was determined through a race, in which the rat cheated by standing on the ox's head and jumping ahead of him when they reached the finish line.

In addition to animals, years are associated with one of the Five Elements: Wood, Fire, Earth, Metal, and Water. Metal years end in zero or one in the lunar calendar; Water years end in two or three; Wood years end in four or five; Fire years end in six or seven; and Earth years end in eight or nine. Thus, depending on the year in which one is born, one might be a Fire Dragon, a Water Dragon, and so on. The full 60 year cycle is a combination of the 12 animals with each of five elements ($12 \times 5 = 60$).

It is a common misconception that there are only the singular animals assigned by year. Many western descriptions of Chinese astrology descriptions draw solely on this system. In fact, you need to look beyond that of your year. You must also take into consideration the inner or month animal, the true or day animal and the secret or hour animal. By combining these four animals together, you are better able to reach a basic analysis of your character. Yet, each animal does not have equal weight in your astrological chart. The year animal has more force than that of the month. The month animal has more weight than that of the day. The day animal is more powerful than that of the hour. Furthermore, the Five Elements should also be taken into consideration. Combined with the Five Elements, this makes for 8,640 possible combinations (five elements, 12 animals, 12 months, 12 times of day) that a person might be. These are all critical for the proper use of Chinese astrology. Many Western displays of the Chinese zodiac omit these, as well as the elements, for easier consumption and understanding.

In the west, there are 12 horoscopes; astrology sees mankind as being not only influenced by hereditary factors and the environment, but also by the state of our solar system at the moment of birth.

Note 1. The 12 zodiac animals (Year animals)

The following are the twelve zodiac signs in order. The first symbol is simply the name of the animal written in Chinese, while the second symbol is the character specifically used in astrology to denote the animal sign.

1) 鼠 子 Rat	2) 牛 丑 Ox	3) 虎 寅 Tiger
4) 兔 卯 Hare	5) 龙 辰 Dragon	6) 蛇 巳 Snake
7) 马 午 Horse	8) 羊 未 Sheep	9) 猴 申 Monkey
10) 鸡 酉 Rooster	11) 狗 戌 Dog	12) 猪 亥 Pig

Note 2. The 12 month animals (Inner Animals)

1) Ox: January	2) Tiger: February	3) Rabbit: March
4) Dragon: April	5) Snake: May	6) Horse: June
7) Sheep: July	8) Monkey: August	9) Rooster: September
10) Dog: October	11) Pig: November	12) Rat: December

Note 3. Day animals (True animals)

Given there are only seven days of the week and 12 animals, there is some repetition or doubling up. The animals for each day are as follows:

1) Monday: Sheep   2) Tuesday: Dragon

3) Wednesday: Horse   4) Thursday: Rat, Pig

5) Friday: Rabbit, Snake, Dog   6) Saturday: Ox, Tiger, Rooster

7) Sunday: Monkey

Note 4. Hour animals (Secret animals)

1) 11am-1am: Rat (The rat is the most active in this period of the day.)

2) 1am-3am: Ox (The ox brings food back from their stomach into their mouth and chews it again in this period of the day.)

3) 3am-5am: Tiger (The tiger hunts preys and is the fiercest in this period of the day.)

4) 5am-7am: Rabbit (The rabbit searches for food in this period of the day.)

5) 7am-9am: Dragon (It's a good time for the dragon to summon the rain.)

6) 9am-11am: Snake (The snake begins to be active in this period of the day.)

7) 11am-1pm: Horse (Yin begins to grow in this period, while horse is a kind of yin animals.)

8) 1pm-3pm: Goat (The goat eats in this period of the day.)

9) 3pm-5pm: Monkey (The monkey is the most active in this period of the day.)

10) 5pm-7pm: Rooster (The rooster begins to return to the chicken coop in this period of the day.)

11) 7pm-9pm: Dog (It's time for the dog to keep watch.)

12) 9pm-11pm: Pig (The pig has sound sleep in this period of the day.)

Note 5. 12 horoscopes

	白羊座 The Ram (March 21st-April 19th) Willpower, impulsive, initiative, courage, energy, activity Often rushes headlong into things		金牛座 The Bull (April 20th-May 20th) Sensual, pleasure-seeker, steadfast, strives for security Sees red when provoked for a long time
	双子座 The Twins (May 21st-June 21st) Mental type, witty, communicative, mobile, takes pleasure in learning. Rarely touches down		巨蟹座 The Crab (June 22nd-July 22nd) Emotional type, stubborn, seeks safety and closeness Very much a family person
	狮子座 The Lion (July 23rd-August 22nd) Glamour, generosity, organizer, the center of attention Likes to take the lion's part		处女座 The Maiden (August 23rd-September 22nd) Precise, differentiates, does what is necessary, utilitarian A critical point of view
	天秤座 The Scales (September 23rd-October 23rd) A sense of beauty and proportion, tactful, seeks balance and harmony. Sometimes hovers between the scales		天蝎座 The Scorpion (October 24th-November 22nd) Corrosive, passionate, piercing, extreme situations Frequently quarrels with the spirits he called
	射手座 The Archer (November 23rd-December 21st) Free spirit, carefree, love of movement, cheerful Wanderlust, often seems to be elsewhere		摩羯座 The Sea Goat (December 22nd-January 19th) Enduring, has a sense of purpose, proud, ambitious Can get stuck in craggy heights

	水瓶座 The Water Bearer (January 20th-February 18th) Communicative, humanitarian, progressive, fraternal Universal spirit with occasional astonishing obstinacy		双鱼座 The Fish (February 19th-March 20th) Sensitive, compassionate, helpful, sociable Very adaptable, hard to get a hold on

3.9 The Main Hall of Zixiao Palace

Now we come to the main building—Zixiao Hall. The hall was built in 1413 and has been repaired more than 10 times. In 1994, the experts from the UN praised, "Here we see an example of repairing ancient architectures in traditional ways." On the roof ridges, there are 61 ornaments such as dragon, phoenix, and immortals, etc.

What is it that gives China's building unmistakable Chinese characteristics? It is the combination of the massive, often curved roof, the extensive use of timber, terrace, and dazzlingly colorful decoration. (1) The roofs of Chinese temples and palaces lend an air of weightlessness to the generally large and massive buildings. The slightly upturned eaves seem to let the entire roof float above the building as if carried on invisible columns. Another way of achieving this illusion of floating is the double roof. Here the roof is constructed in two stages and the low wall separating the two suggests a small additional story. A practical function of upturned roof gutters is to ensure enough light inside the building while making it easy to carry off rain water. Additionally, the roofs of palaces are covered with glazed tiles. As the emperor's color was yellow, those of the imperial palace are in yellow. The Temple of Heaven, on the other hand, is appropriately covered with blue tiles, the color of the sky. (2) Visitors who see Chinese buildings will notice the extensive use of timber as a building material in addition to bricks and tiles. That is because timber was not only easily available and transportable but also was very practical. Heavy posts are capable of carrying the roof while the wood could be carved for decoration and embellishment. (3) Buildings in China, whether temples, palaces or pagodas, rise invariably from a terrace. That is as it should be, for the wooden frame, no matter how flexible it is, has to be protected from any ingress of water. The terrace in these terms represents the Earth and the roof the Heaven. Thus we come to the recurrent theme of ancient Chinese philosophy, which is a complete harmony between man and nature. All these give a clue to the social status of the palaces and the temples because ordinary people were not permitted to have them: they were the prerogative of people of rank.

We can see three plaques made during the reign of Emperor Jiajing and Chenghua in the Ming Dynasty. In 1995, Taiwanese pilgrims donated money to gild the Chinese characters. In the middle is "Yun Wai Qing Du"（云外清都）; "Yun" means clouds, "Wai" means above, "Qing Du" means the peaceful palace, so the four characters mean the peaceful palace above the clouds. Zixiao Palace has the best Fengshui, so it is regarded as the peaceful palace above the clouds, which reflects the Taoist ideology of holding oneself aloof from the world. "Shi Pan Liu Tian"（始判六天）and "Xie Zan Zhong Tian"（协赞中天）mean that at the very beginning, the world was a dark void, God Ziwei and Emperor Zhenwu helped the Jade Emperor stamp out the demons on Wudang Mountain and keep the world in order.

Let's look at the couplets. There are more than 3,000 plaques and couplets and the ones here are of great importance. One is "金殿重辉看鸟革翚（huī）飞势化山河维社稷，帝容复整仰龙章凤姿光同日月炳乾坤." The right one means that the repaired hall look imposing and magnificent, which indicates that the nation is prosperous and people live a stable and rich life (the hall was repaired during the reign of Emperor Jiajing in the Ming Dynasty). The left one means that Emperor Zhenwu is worshiped by people; he is compared to the sun and the moon bringing sunshine to all the people. The other is "三世有缘人涉水登山朝圣境，一声无量佛惊天动地振玄都." The right one means that the lucky person has the opportunity to hike up Wudang Mountain; the luckier person has the opportunity to live on Wudang Mountain and the luckiest person has the opportunity to be buried on Wudang Mountain. The left one means pilgrims murmur prayers, which moves Emperor Zhenwu and the blessing of Emperor Zhenwu falls upon all of them.

Now we have entered the hall. It is supported by 36 pillars, representing 36 Tiangang（天罡）, the stars forming the handle of the Big Dipper（北斗星的斗柄）. In the middle is the statue of Emperor Zhenwu. With a height of 4.8 meters, the image is the biggest clay sculpture on Wudang Mountain. He wears Mian Liu（冕旒）on his head and holds Xiang Hu（相笏）in his hand. Mian Liu can only be used by the Jade Emperor, the supreme god in the minds of Chinese. Xiang Hu is used by ministers. So the statue shows that Zhenwu holds the position next to the Jade Emperor. Below it is also a statue of Emperor Zhenwu. We can see he is holding a sword. These two statues show that Zhenwu is both a civilian and a military officer. Beside the statue of Emperor Zhenwu, we can also see a boy and a girl, they are called Golden Boy and Jade Girl respectively. Now Golden Boy and Jade Girl usually refer to the perfect partner in the field of entertainment. The statues on both sides we can see here are of Emperor Zhenwu made in different dynasties.

The left niche houses a paper-pasted but gilded statue of Emperor Zhenwu, made in the 17th century. It is 0.89 meters high and 0.26 meters wide. This is the earliest discovered and most well preserved paper joss of the whole nation so far. This sculpture was mistaken as bronze gilded till April 13th, 2003, when the staff members conducted an investigation of the relics here. The wonderful thing is that the statue does not peel off and has not been bitten by worm inside.

Here we can see a fir log, about 10 meters long. Its diameter is about 0.3 meters. Legend says it flew here, so it's called "flying fir." Strike the log from one side, and you can hear it from the other side; it's also called "echoing fir." Some say if you hear the echo, you will be lucky, so it is also called "lucky fir." Many people have struck the log, and two several-centimeter-deep holes have formed, so it is kept inside so that no one is allowed to strike it any more.

Let's look at the couplets.(1) "屏（bǐng）红尘以悟道机神静元真觉才成此极天蟠（pán）地文章；去皇宫而岩穴木石居鹿豕（shǐ）游因做这超前轶后事业." The couplet tells us that Zhenwu, a crown prince, gave up the comfortable life and refined himself in a terrible situation. At last, he succeeded and flew to Heaven. (2) "跣（xiǎn）足云为履游三界踏破真空佛号西无量佛，披发天作冠荫九洲覆昌实境道称北极至尊." This couplet means that Emperor Zhenwu traveled around the world with his hair falling over his shoulder, bare-foot and with the clouds as his ride. In Taoism, Zhenwu is regarded as the god of the north; in Buddhism, he is respected as Amitabha（佛）.

3.10 Yunshuitang Hall

Yunshuitang Hall, the office of Taoism Association, was once a place for the deans of different halls to negotiate over major events. On May 26th, 1999, Jiang Zemin, the former Chairman of PRC, had an interview with the head of the Taoism Association. After watching a wushu performance and listening to Taoist music, Jiang Zemin also practiced Tai Chi Quan here.

On the wall we can see Jing Zhu Mao Zhu Xi Wan Shou Wu Jiang （敬祝毛主席万寿无疆！）, which means "May Chairman Mao live long!" These were written by Red Guards（红卫兵）during the Cultural Revolution (1966-1976). Red Guards thought pilgrims were superstitious and the statues of gods should be damaged. When Red Guards came to Wudang Mountain, the State Council issued an order that the cultural relics should be protected, so the Red Guards left Wudang Mountain.

This is Shangshan Pool（上善池）. Shangshan means the highest good. In Lao Tzu's *Tao Te Ching*, there is a saying that the highest good is like water which benefits all things and contends with none. In Taoist tradition, water is considered an aspect of wisdom. The concept here is that water takes on the form in which it is held and moves in the path of least resistance. Here the symbolic meaning of water speaks of a higher wisdom we may all aspire to mimic.

Here we can see one of the wonders on Wudang Mountain: Spraying water out of the stone tortoise's neck. There is a legend: The tortoise used to steal the sacrifices to Emperor Zhenwu. One day, Emperor Zhenwu found it and ordered the tortoise to disgorge them. But the tortoise was so stubborn that he refused to do that. Irritated, Emperor Zhenwu took out his sword and cut its head off its neck. In fact, the true reason is that the rock was disintegrated by frost and rain.

Jin Yin Sha Keng（金银沙坑）: There are two pits. Legend has it that the one who donates a lot to Wudang Mountain can get a handful of golden sand, the one who donates less can get a handful of silver sand, the one who donates none can only get a handful of sand.

3.11 Roof of the Main Hall

Outside the hall, we can see six flying colored glazed dragons with a vase in the middle. In Buddhism, the vase symbolizes wealth and teaches us that we should enjoy the inner wealth of our faith, moral discipline, our study, benefiting others, consideration for others, and wisdom. The vase is drawn by four iron chains and each end of the chain is attached to the hand of a child. It is said that the four children stick to their positions in order to keep the vase steady no matter how bad the weather is. Because their spatial positions are even higher than the superior god, the four kids are also called "Super Immortals". However, the locals call them "Wretched Kids"（苦娃）, for they have to be exposed to the weather, suffering unpleasant experiences all the year round.

Look at the both ends of the roof ridge, the animal-shaped parts are called Chiwen（螭吻）, one of Dragon's children. They are used to decorate the roof and prevent water from entering the hall.

Can you see three deities? "Fu Lu Shou" refers to the concept of Good Fortune (Fu), Prosperity (Lu), and Longevity (Shou). Traditionally, they are arranged from right to left (so Fu is on the right of the viewer, Lu in the middle, and Shou on the far left). According to Taoist legend, the Fu star is associated with Yang Cheng （阳城）, a governor of Daozhou（道州）. Yang Cheng risked his life by advising the emperor that the dwarfs should not be sent to the court as a tribute. After his death, the people built a temple to commemorate him, and over time he came to be considered the personification of good fortune. He is generally depicted in scholar's dress, holding a scroll, on which is sometimes written the character "Fu". He may also be seen holding a child, or surrounded by children. The word "Lu" specifically refers to the salary of a government official. As such, the Lu star is the star of prosperity, rank, and influence. The Lu star was also worshiped as the deity dictating one's success in the imperial examinations, and therefore success in the imperial bureaucracy. The Lu star is usually depicted in the dress of a mandarin. The Shou star is believed to control the life spans of mortals. According to legend, he was carried in his mother's womb for ten years before being born, and was already an old man when delivered. He is recognized by his high, domed forehead and the peach which he carries as a symbol of immortality. The God of Longevity is usually shown smiling and friendly, and he may sometimes carry a gourd filled with Elixir of Life.

Adapted from http://www.ask.com/wiki/Fu_Lu_Shou?qsrc=3044

Extended Reading 6: The Eight Auspicious Signs in Buddhism

In Taoism, there are eight immortals, whose talismans are called "Hidden Eight Immortals". In Buddhism, there are also eight auspicious signs（佛教八宝）as follows:

The umbrella symbolizes the umbrella of the Buddhist community and teaches us that first we should enter the Buddhist family.	The fish symbolizes harmony indicating that under this umbrella we should always live in harmony and peace.
 The umbrella 宝伞	 The fish 双鱼
The vase symbolizes wealth and wisdom. It teaches us that we should enjoy the inner wealth of our faith, moral discipline, our study and practice of Dharma, benefiting others, sense of shame, consideration for others.	The lotus symbolizes purity which indicates that we should always strive to become a pure being by practicing the Bodhisattva's way of life.

The vase 宝瓶

The lotus 莲花

The conch shell symbolizes the Dharma Jewel and teaches us that we should accomplish the Dharma Jewel, the realizations of the stages of the path, within our mind.

The knot of eternity symbolizes an uncommon quality of Buddha's realizations, namely his realization of omniscient wisdom.

The conch shell 法螺

The knot of eternity 盘长

The victory banner symbolizes an uncommon quality of Buddha's abandonment, his abandonment of the delusions and mistaken appearance.

These last two together (the knot of eternity and the victory banner) indicate that through gaining the Dharma Jewel, the realizations of the stages of the path to enlightenment, we shall attain these two uncommon qualities of Buddha.

The Dharma wheel indicates that, having attained these two uncommon qualities of Buddha, we are able to lead all living beings to permanent liberation from suffering, principally by turning the wheel of Dharma, which is by giving Dharma teachings. This is our final goal.

The victory banner 宝幢

The Dharma wheel 法轮

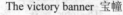

The Buddhist symbols, The Eight Auspicious Signs, are very meaningful religious symbols of Buddhism, revealing our progress along the Buddhist path to enlightenment.

Adapted from http://www.exoticindiaart.com/symbols.htm

3.12 Parent Hall

According to the record, the Parent Hall was first built during the reign of Emperor Yongle in the Ming Dynasty (1403-1424), but damaged later. The existing one was rebuilt at the beginning of the 20th century (in the early period of the Republic of China, 民国初期）. It is a three-story building, made of wood and bricks.

The Parent Halls can be found in all large palaces on Wudang Mountain, which is one of the significant characteristics of Taoism architectures of Wudang Mountain. In the Ming Dynasty, Taoism was divided into two sects, Quanzhen and Zhengyi. Quanzhen Taoism is distinguished by its practice of Inner Alchemy（内丹）, requirement of a monastic lifestyle and its unification of Buddhism, Confucianism and Taoism and its lineage tracing back to Wang Chongyang（王重阳）. Zhengyi Taoism distinguishes itself by practicing talismans and living a non-monastic lifestyle and its lineage tracing back to Zhang

Daoling（张道陵）. Wang Chongyang advocated filial piety, which changed the old practice that monks or nuns should have nothing to do with their relatives or friends. Therefore, the Parent Hall was a place to educate people to be filial to parents. Do you know why the Parent Hall is always built at the back of the Main Hall? Because whatever we do, we can be supported by our parents.

There are three shrines inside the hall. The statues of Emperor Zhenwu's parents, Emperor Mingzhen and Queen Shansheng, who were called "Saint Father" and "Saint Mother" by Taoist monks, were worshiped in the middle shrine. The couplet "父生天天长地久，母生地地久天长" means that Zhenwu's parents are compared to Heaven and Earth; both of them can live eternally.

On the right is Goddess of Mercy. In Taoism, she is called "慈航道人". "Guanyin" is short for "Guanshiyin", which means "to witness and listen to the prayers and cries of those in difficulty." Guanyin is an extremely popular Goddess in Chinese folk belief and is worshiped in China due to her unconditional love, compassion and mercy. In China, Guanyin is usually shown in a white flowing robe and usually wears necklaces. In her left hand is a vase containing pure water, and the right holds a willow branch. (According to textual research, the willow branch functioned as toothbrush, and it was believed that the water could free people from troubles.) But before the Song Dynasty (960-1279), representations of Guanyin in China were masculine in appearance. Later, it was regarded as disgraceful when many women also worshiped Guanyin in the form of men at home; the images displaying attributes of both genders came into being. Besides, Guanyin also has the power to grant children. Because of the personification of compassion and kindness, a mother-goddess and patron of mothers and seamen, the representation in China was further interpreted in an all-female form around the 12th century. In the Tang Dynasty, Guanshiyin changed to Guanyin due to the naming taboo of Emperor Gaozong of Tang, who is called Li Shimin.

On the left are the statues of three goddesses. There is a couplet: "三光映瑞群仙殿，霄云起祥百子堂，" which means that the hall, bathed in sunlight, houses the goddesses, who can help the married couple without children realize their dream.

This was once He Long's office. In 1931, He Long（贺龙）, a famous revolutionist, came here with many injured soldiers. Xu Benshan（徐本善）, a Taoist Master at that time, ordered the other Taoist monks to search for medical herbs to cure the injured and risk their lives to get food for the soldiers in the KMT-occupied area.

3.13 Crown Prince Cave

Behind Zixiao Palace lies Zhanqi Peak. At the end of the ancient stone steps is Crown Prince Cave. Crown Prince Cave was built in the early Yuan Dynasty (1206-1368). Being quiet and far away from the outside world, it is a good place for refinement. Now we have come to Crown Prince Cave, a natural den. It is said that Zhenwu, Crown Prince of State Jingle, once refined here.

IV. Nanyan Scenic Zone

4.1 Introduction

Nanyan Palace is 2.5 km away from Zixiao Palace. It is also called "Southern Crag Palace", since it faces south. Nanyan Palace was not built according to the traditional rule that buildings should be arranged symmetrically; ancient craftsmen made good use of the mountain's topography, achieving a high degree of harmony with the surroundings. Since 1996, it has been listed as one of National Key Cultural Relics Protecting Units by State Council.

Since the 7th century, people have refined themselves here. It was said that Lv Dongbin once refined himself and wrote a poem here. 1413 saw a large-scale construction of the buildings. However, they were damaged at the end of the 19th century.

Look at the palace built into the side of the cliff. Is it a wonder? This style is also used in Buddhism architectures, such as Xuankong Temple（悬空寺，Hanging Temple）in Datong City, Shanxi Province. Its purpose is to make it imposing, beautiful and mysterious.

4.2 Taichang Temple

Taichang Temple is always surrounded by clouds and fog, so it is also called Yunxia Temple (Cloud-Fog Temple). Why is it called Taichang? It is said that a Taoist named Taichang lived on Wudang Mountain. Once he cured the emperor's mother and refused all the rewards. Because of this, the emperor ordered to build a temple on Wudang Mountain in the name of this Taoist so that he would be remembered by later generations. Another version is that the construction of the temple was supervised by Ren Ziyuan, a Taichang, which is an official rank.

On the screen wall, we can see Lao Tzu on a black cow. This is a very famous idiom—Zi Qi Dong Lai（紫气东来）. Zi means purple, Qi means cloud, Dong Lai means coming eastward. Yinxi, the head of Hanguguan Pass（函谷关）, saw purple clouds drifting from the east, and then predicted a saint would pass here. When Lao Tzu came here on a black cow, he immediately knelt down hoping that Lao Tzu would enlighten him. Lao Tzu thought Yinxi was sincere, so he lived there and wrote a 5,000-word book. That is *Tao Te Ching* (*Classic of the Way and its Power*), Lao Tzu's biggest achievement. It consists of two parts: Daojing, with an emphasis on philosophy, and Dejing, with an emphasis on politics and military affairs. *Tao Te Ching* played a key role in the formation of ancient Chinese philosophy. It is said that after finishing this book, Lao Tzu was never seen again.

The screen wall, called Yingbi（影壁）or Zhaobi（照壁）in Chinese, can be made of any kind of material—brick, wood, stone or glazed tile. In ancient times, the screen wall was built to prevent ghosts from entering the hall. According to the theory of Fengshui, it's not good if Qi enters the hall, so a wall was built. For the sake of ventilation, the wall is not closed.

In the middle of the hall is a 1.96-meter-high statue of Lao Tzu. The goddess of the Big Dipper's Mother（斗姆）is also worshiped. She has three eyes, four heads, and four arms on each side, with the weapons of the sun, the moon, along with a bow and an arrow in her hands.

4.3 Thunder God Cave

This is Lei Gong Cave (the Thunder God Cave). The reason why people worshiped the Thunder God was that ancient people were in awe of thunder and lightning. In Chinese mythology, the Thunder God is the Chinese Taoist deity who punishes both earthly mortals guilty of secret crimes and evil spirits who have used their knowledge of Taoism to harm human beings. The Thunder God carries a drum and mallet to produce thunder and a chisel to punish evildoers.

Temples dedicated to the Thunder God are rare, but some people honor him in hope that he will take revenge on their personal enemies. The cave is the only place to worship the Thunder God on Wudang Mountain. In the cave is the statue of Lei Gong carved in the Ming Dynasty, the biggest one on Wudang Mountain. He is depicted as a fearsome creature with claws, bat wings, and a blue face with a bird's beak who wears only a loincloth.

According to history, the cave was built in the Ming Dynasty. Zhang Shouqing, a famous Wudang Mountain Taoist, refined himself and prayed for rain here.

Behind the cave, there is a natural spring, streaming all the year round. Cool in summer, warm in winter and having a sweet taste, it is also called "Supernatural Spring"（灵池）.

4.4 Nanyan Pagoda

Now we can see a pagoda, which originated from Buddhism. They were originally supposed to keep relics of the Buddha, scriptures and ritual instruments. Can you see a Yin-Yang Diagram of the Supreme Ultimate, a symbol of Taoism? We know the pagoda is for a Taoist monk. When a monk dies, he will be put in a jar, and filled with charcoal, lime and perfumes to preserve the body. Then the jar will be sealed. Finally, a pagoda will be built over the jar. The higher the pagoda is，the higher status the dead Taoist enjoys. This practice can be found both in Buddhism and Taoism. This method is called Zuo Gang（坐缸, sitting in the jar）. It is still used by some pious Buddhists and Taoists. Why is the method used? Because a monk wants to show he is different from an ordinary person, who usually dies lying down. In addition, it can indicate that he approaches death calmly and peacefully.

The oldest existing pagoda, also built of wood, is located in Yingxian County（应县）in north Shanxi. It was a miracle that the 67.13-meter-high pagoda should have survived all the vicissitudes of life for more than 900 years, including some strong earthquakes. Because it is out of the way, most visitors do not see this pagoda. More frequently visited pagodas are the Great Wild Goose Pagoda （大雁塔）in Xi'an, the Pagoda of Six Harmonies（六和塔）in Hangzhou, and the Forest of Pagodas（塔林）near Shaolin Monastery in Henan, central China, to name just a few.

4.5 Small Celestial Gate

Here we have come to Xiao Tian Men (Small Celestial Gate, 小
天门). Do you know how to read the symbol? In the Tang Dynasty,
Empress Wu Zetian defined the pronunciation of the symbol as
"Wan". We have the clockwise swastika and the counter-clockwise
sauvastika. Some believe the symbols mean differently: the clockwise
one, symbolizing health and life, is used as a good luck sign while the
counter-clockwise one takes on a meaning of being strong and solid.
Some think they are interchangeable; the difference is caused by
observing the symbol from different angles. Religious version takes
the shape of a square, while Nazi version has a cross in the middle
and takes the shape of a rhombus. It means hate, violence, death, and
murder. There was a time when Premier Zhou Enlai treated some
foreigners to a dish with the sign. Confused by the religious and Nazi
version, the foreigners asked Premier Zhou why the Chinese used the
sign to make the dish. Premier Zhou explained it and said that it
could be eaten even if it was regarded as Nazi emblem.

4.6 Imperial Tablet Pavilion

This is an Imperial Tablet Pavilion. There are 12 pavilions
altogether: two in Jingle Palace in Danjiangkou City, two in Zixiao
Palace, two in Nanyan Palace, two in Five-Dragon Palace and four in
Yuxu Palace. Usually pavilions come in pairs; this is the only place
where two pavilions don't stand opposite each other. The heaviest

one is 102 tons and 8.5 meters high; it's in the city of Danjiangkou. But here we can see only one pavilion. It is 75 tons and was built in 1412. It recorded the rules for a Taoist. A Taoist is required to empty his mind. If he breaks the rules, he will be driven away from Wudang Mountain, or be seriously punished. How were the steles erected? The method is called Tu Tun（土囤法）. First, they built the base, and then heaped up the earth with a hole in the middle to hold the stele. After that, they lifted the stele up the hill until it could be put into the hole.

4.7 Ginkgo Tree

Now we have come to the entrance to Nanyan Palace. On Wudang Mountain, there are more than 500 kinds of plants under state protection. Can you guess the age of the tree? It is 750 years old. Most of ginkgo trees can live 3,500 years; in China, there are 12 which are more than 5,000 years old. Besides, it grows extremely slowly; it takes 20 years for this kind of tree to begin to grow fruits and 40 years to grow a large number of fruits. If a grandfather plants the tree, the tree will not bear fruits until the grandson generation, so it's also called "Grandfather-Grandson tree". The Ginkgo is a living fossil, dating back 270 million years. What surprises us most is that several ginkgo trees have survived the atomic bombs dropped in Japan in the Second World War.

Ginkgo is an herb. The list of uses of ginkgo is very long. This may be because this herb has been around for so long. Ginkgo is often used for memory disorders. It is also used for conditions that stem from reduced blood flow in the brain, especially in older people. These conditions include memory loss, headache, ringing in the ears, difficulty concentrating and hearing disorders. Some people use it for other problems related to poor blood flow in the body, including leg pain when walking, and a painful response to cold, especially in the fingers and toes. In manufacturing, ginkgo leaf extract is used in cosmetics. In foods, roasted ginkgo seed, which has the pulp removed, is an edible delicacy in Japan and China. Remember, though, the unrefined leaf and seed are likely unsafe to eat.

4.8 Tiger Rock

Can you see a footprint? Legend has it that it was made by Emperor Zhenwu. When Emperor Zhenwu refined himself here, a rock was going to fall because of a heavy rain. At this moment, Zhenwu used one of his feet to support it and that's the footprint we can see now. On the rock is a 600-word carving recording the military training of the KMT troops at Wudang Mountain in 1939.

4.9 Incense Burner

There is also an incense burner. In order to avoid fire in temples, incense burners were built outside temples for pilgrims to burn incense. This burner was built in the Yuan Dynasty. Until 2008, nobody dared to repair the incense burner for lack of technology.

4.10 Dragon-Tiger Hall

This is Dragon-Tiger Hall. When being opened, the door will

produce a great sound. It is believed that the pilgrims hearing the sound will be lucky.

4.11 Xuandi Hall

This is Xuandi Hall, a major hall of Nanyan Palace. It's a restoration. Nanyan Palace was first built in the Yuan Dynasty and in the early 15th century (1403-1424). Unluckily, Xuandi Hall was destroyed in a fire. In 1926, some Taoist monks finished their evening exercises and were leaving the hall with a kerosene lamp. But the kerosene lamp fell; one of the Taoist monks kicked the lamp hoping to put out the fire. Instead of putting out the lamp fire, a big fire broke out. They tried to put it out with the well water, but it did not work and the hall was in ruins.

In 2004, with the permission of State Cultural Relics Bureau and the total investment of 7 million yuan, Hubei Provincial Government began to rebuild the hall. The blueprint was made by Wang Guixiang （王贵祥）, professor from Qinghua University. When rebuilding the hall, the first problem was how to transport the materials to the site. The solution is the cableway, so less than 300 workers were employed to build the hall. The second problem was painting. It took up one fourth of the whole project. The painter is called Zhou Changming（周长明）from Henan Province. He and his men needed to spend 10 hours every day painting on the scaffold. Also the lighting has to be dim, because too strong lighting may weaken the colors.

Now we have entered the hall. In the middle is the statue of Emperor Zhenwu. On each side are the statues of Golden Boy and

Jade Girl. Below are the statues of the four law-protecting gods in Taoism. Glass is used to protect the original ground.

4.12 Inscriptions of Fu, Shou, Kang and Ning

We can see four Chinese characters "Fu, Shou, Kang and Ning." People thought they were written by Wang Yong（王顒）. But in fact, after observing carefully, we can find they have different styles. According to experts, Shou was written by Wang Yong in 1537. The other three Chinese characters were written by Xia Yan（夏言）in 1542. Let me tell you the story. Xia Yan, a high-ranked official, knew that Emperor Jiajing believed in Taoism. In order to show his loyalty to the emperor, he wrote Tian Zi Wan Nian（天子万年，May the emperor live as long as Emperor Zhenwu) and sent Wang Yong to Wudang Mountain with the four characters. After worshiping Emperor Zhenwu, Wang Yong also wrote Shou（寿, longevity）and had it carved here. After knowing this, Emperor Jiajing appreciated Xia Yan and gave him a promotion. Emperor Jiajing also bestowed a cap especially for a Taoist monk upon him, but he refused to wear the cap during the audiences with the emperor. Framed and cashiered, Xia Yan realized that happiness, peace and health were the most important. So he wrote Fu (happiness), Kang (health) and Ning (peace) and had them sent to Wudang Mountain.

4.13 Inscriptions of Nan Yan

Anther two Chinese characters are: Nan Yan. Yan is made up of two Chinese characters. On the top is Pin（品）, below it is Shan（山）.

Pin means appreciate and Shan means mountain. Yan means we should admire the scenery and appreciate Wudang Mountain from the bottom of our hearts.

4.14 Scripture Hall

This is Scripture Hall. It is said that Chen Tuan, a famous Taoist monk in early Song Dynasty, once refined here. By imitating animals' hibernation in winter, he could sleep for several months or years. There is a story about him. One day, a farmer saw a body covered with a lot of dust. The farmer was sympathetic and planned to bury it. When dusting it, the farmer realized it was a living man. The man opened his eyes and asked, "Why did you wake me up?"

On the walls of Scripture Hall, we can see two sidelong Chinese characters written by Chen Tuan "Fu（福）and Shou（寿）", which mean happiness and longevity respectively. In China, the two characters written by him can be found in many scenic spots, such as Anyue（安岳）, Dazhu（大足）, Tongnan（潼南）, Emeishan（峨眉山）and Huashan（华山）.

4.15 Liangyi Hall

Liangyi Hall（两仪殿）is also called "Parent Hall". Liangyi refers to Yin and Yang, Heaven and Earth. According to the *Book of Changes*, Heaven refers to father and Earth refers to mother, so here Emperor Zhenwu's parents are worshiped here. In the west are three goddesses. The couples who want to have babies usually pray here.

In the east are the Three Pure Ones（三清）, the highest gods in

Taoism. They are regarded as pure manifestation of the Tao and the origin of all sentient beings. In Tao produces One—Wuji produces Taiji, it means the Universe was still null and the cosmos was in disorder; manifesting into the first of the Taoist Trinity, Yuanshi Tianzun（元始天尊）, who oversaw the earliest phase of Creation of the Universe. In One produces Two—Taiji produces Yin and Yang, Yuanshi Tianzun manifests into Lingbao Tianzun（灵宝天尊）who separated the Yang from the Yin, the clear from the murky, and classified the elements into their rightful groups. In the final phase of Creation, Daode Tianzun（道德天尊）is manifested from Lingbao Tianzun to bring civilization and preach the Law to all living beings. Each of them holds onto a divine object associated with their task. Yuanshi Tianzun is usually depicted holding the Pearl of Creation（丹丸）, signifying his role in creating the Universe from void and chaos. The Ruyi（如意）held by Lingbao Tianzun represents the second phase of Creation where the Yang was separated from the Yin and the Law of Things was put in place. Lingbao Tianzun then took his seat on the left of Yuanshi Tianzun. Later, when all was complete, Daode Tianzun took his place on the right, with the fan symbolizing the completion of Creation, and the act of fanning represents the spreading of Tao to all Mankind.

4.16 Dragon-Head Incense Burner

In Nanyan Palace, there is a protruding stone sculpture, called Dragon-Head Incense Burner. Dragon-Head Incense Burner faces the Golden Hall, just like paying religious homage. It's 3 meters long and

0.55 meters wide. In fact, it is two dragons carved together by ancient craftsmen. On the head of the dragon, there is an incense burner, under which is a deep valley.

Legend has it that it was these two huge dragons that Zhenwu often traveled on. Because of its mystical status, many people in the past risked their lives to burn incense here to show their piety. It was so dangerous that thousands of people died, so in 1673 (during the reign of Emperor Kangxi in the Qing Dynasty), people were forbidden to burn incense here.

The Parent Hall, Dragon-Head stone and the Golden Hall are in the same line. Liangyi Hall is a place to honor Zhenwu's parents. People give sacrifices here hoping that whatever they do, they can be supported by their parents. People also hope to express their gratitude and reverence through the rising smoke.

4.17 Stone Hall

In Nanyan Palace, the most famous architecture is Tianyi Zhenqing Stone Hall（天乙真庆宫）. It's said that after Zhenwu ascended to Heaven, the place he lived in Heaven is called Tianyi Zhenqing Hall, so Zhenwu's followers built the hall on the earth.

The stone hall was built in the Yuan Dynasty, when the imperial rulers bestowed great favors upon Taoism and Wudang Mountain became a grand service of the imperial court to pray for longevity and consecration. Wudang Taoism also had great influence on the common people so that thousands of Taoist followers in the country made pilgrimages to Wudang Mountain every year. Zhang Shouqing came to Wudang Mountain in 1284. He and his disciples took advantage of the situation and spent 27 years building the palace. In 1312 and 1313, there was a heavy drought in the capital (Beijing); Zhang Shouqing was summoned to pray for rain. He succeeded and was granted a lot including the horizontal inscribed board.

This stone hall has a mortise-and-tenon structure. The roof beams, pillars, square timbers, windows, doors, joints and animal sculptures on the roof ridges were all made of stone and then joined together. In 1990, some experts regarded this stone hall as one of the masterpieces of ancient Chinese architecture and a representative of ancient Chinese stone buildings.

In the middle is a statue of Emperor Zhenwu and below it are the statues of Si Yu（四御）, the gods just next to the Three Pure Ones in Taoism. On each side are the statues of military and civilian Zhenwu. The small statues are of 500 soldiers. Legend has it that when Zhenwu, a crown prince of State Jingle, came to Wudang Mountain at the age of 15, his mother followed him here with 500 soldiers, who knelt down in the hope that Emperor Zhenwu would change his mind and return home. Determined to continue his refinement, Emperor Zhenwu cast a spell on the soldiers. Then the soldiers turned motionless except for their mouth. After the soldiers expressed their willingness to stay here, they returned to normal. When Zhenwu became an immortal, they were also promoted to guardian deities. Before the statue is a box in which books recording donators' names are put.

4.18 Bed with Crown Prince Lying on

Here we can see a statue of a crown prince lying on a bed. Let me tell you the myth. It is said Zhenwu refined himself here for a long time, but achieved nothing. He was still troubled by the worldly life. His master granted him a dragon-head crutch, so he decided to sleep with it to empty his mind. After Zhenwu became an immortal, dragon-head crutches were popular with the Taoists who wanted to keep peace of mind.

4.19 Flying-to-Heaven Cliff

Flying-to-Heaven Cliff is the place where Emperor Zhenwu refined himself and went up to Heaven. It is said that on the day of March 3rd of the lunar calendar, Zhenwu would fly to Heaven. God Ziqi, his master, wanted to know whether he was qualified enough to go up to Heaven, so he went to help Zhenwu comb his hair in the form of a beautiful girl. But Zhenwu kept away from her. This made the beautiful girl feel ashamed, so she jumped to death from here. Without hesitation, Zhenwu risked his life to save the beautiful girl. At that time, five dragons appeared and supported Zhenwu up to Heaven.

A Dressing Table on Flying Cliff was built according to this legend. Outside the Dressing Table, there is a large stone named Shixinshi（试心石）. It is said that Zhenwu dived from this stone and then flew to Heaven. Below the stone is a deep abyss.

Extended Reading 7: Children of Dragon

The Chinese dragon is a benevolent creature that saved

mankind from drought by making it rain. The dragon also has the power to calm waters, so when a river floods, a dragon is called upon to dispel the waters. There are nine different young of the dragon, whose shapes are used as ornaments according to their nature within Chinese mythology.

(1) Bixi（赑屃）actually has a tortoise shape, but is considered to be one of the dragon legends. Bixi is frequently carved as the base for important memorials. (2) Chiwen（螭吻/鸱吻）is seen on top of things. If you look at the roof-ridge of a building, his image is often carved there so he can gaze into the distance and provide early warning. (3) Pulao（蒲牢）is fond of his own voice and likes to roar, so his image is carved on bells. (4) Bi'an（狴犴）guards the gates of prisons. Bi'an is the law and order type and therefore the symbol of litigation. (5) Baxia（霸下）is most often found near water. His image will be carved on bridges and arches leading to piers so that he can take a swim when he likes and protect the travelers from the water. (6) Yazi（睚眦/睚眥）can be found engraved on the handles of knives and the hilts of swords. Yazi is brave and belligerent. (7) Suanni（狻猊）is fond of smoke and fire, so he twines up the legs of incense-burners. Suanni, which likes to sit down, is represented upon the bases of Buddhist idols (under the Buddhas' or Bodhisattvas' feet). (8) Taotie （饕餮）loves to eat and is found on food-related wares. (9) Jiaotu（椒图）can keep his mouth shut like a clam. He appears as either a conch spiral shape or a clamshell shape. He is found on door lintels, front doors, and major entryways. He guards your peace and privacy.

V. On the Way to the Palace of Supreme Harmony

5.1 Betelnut-Plum Temple

Betelnut-Plum Temple was built in Emperor Yongle's tenth year in the Ming Dynasty (1412).

There is a legend about Zhenwu in this place. It is said that Zhenwu refined himself on Wudang Mountain for a long time, but he achieved nothing, so he wanted to give up. On the way home, he met an old lady, who told him that perseverance spells success. In fact, the old lady was his master, God Ziqi. He returned and continued his practice. When passing the place, he broke off one plum branch, stuck it into a betel nut tree, and said, "If the tree can blossom, it means I will be successful." Later, the tree blossomed and yielded fruits, and he succeeded, too.

Betelnut-plum fruits on Wudang Mountain had a very high reputation in the Ming Dynasty. During the reign of Yongle (1403-1425), Li Suxi（李素希）, a Taoist, presented them to the emperor and the emperor was very happy, because the fruits were not only delicious but also good for health. The emperor demanded the fruits should be sent to the imperial court as a tribute, and the emperor rewarded his outstanding officials with the fruits. Those officials who received the fruits regarded it as a political credit and were happy. Then the emperor ordered the construction of Betelnut-Plum Temple. After the temple was completed, the betelnut-plum trees died away, and no one could explain the reason. Luckily, in 1526, when a Taoist from the Qiyun Mountain, Anhui Province, came to Wudang Mountain, the Taoists on Wudang Mountain sent him a betlenut-plum tree as a gift. In 1997, the government transplanted a betelnut-plum tree from Qiyun Mountain to Wudang Mountain and in 2004, the tree grew 6 fruits.

Did Zhenwu really stick a plum branch into a betel nut tree? No. This is just a legend. How to explain it scientifically? Some experts think that birds eat plums on betel nut trees and the stone falls into the crevice of the betel nut trees, so a new kind of fruit comes into being.

Here we can see the statues of Zhenwu, the Jade Emperor（玉皇大帝）and other officials. In China, it is well known that the Jade Emperor is the most powerful dominator. He is in charge of all kinds of traditional gods belonging to Buddhism and Taoism. His birthday falls on January 9 of the lunar calendar, when a grand ceremony is held.

5.2 Yellow Dragon Cave

Yellow Dragon Cave is situated on the way to the Golden Hall. On Wudang Mountain, Yellow Dragon Cave is connected with Taoist medicines, such as Yellow Dragon Cave Eye Ointment（眼药膏）, etc., which are historically renowned in the history. On the upper side of

Yellow Dragon Cave are four tablets, on two of which are four Chinese characters "Tian Xia Chi Ming（天下驰名）", which means "Famous in the world", showing the medicines made on Wudang Mountain are very famous. On the other two tablets are the uses of the medicines and what diseases the medicines can cure.

In the 14th and 15th centuries (the Ming Dynasty), Taoists took advantage of the cave to cure diseases. A rope fastened to a small basket was connected with the pavilion below Yellow Dragon Cave. Those who wanted to buy the medicine can put money in the basket and then ring the bell. Thus, the basket would be pulled up by the Taoists in the cave and lowered with the medicine later, so the person who wanted to buy the medicine did not see the doctor and seller. Here we can see a stone stele, which is regarded as the commercial advertisement in the Ming Dynasty left on Wudang Mountain.

The most outstanding feature of the cave is that it contains many smaller caves inside. According to legend, one yellow dragon refined itself here and ascended to Heaven. To show its appreciation to the cave, it left a panacea（万能药）in the spring to cure all the diseases. The palace and statue were constructed to show people's admiration and thanks to the yellow dragon.

It is recorded that many Taoists refined themselves here before the Song Dynasty. In ancient times, men who made a pilgrimage to Wudang Mountain firmly believed that if they entered Yellow Dragon Cave, they would be very lucky.

5.3 Heavenward Temple

Heavenward Temple is built on the way to the Golden Hall. It is 1,400 meters above sea level. Emperor Yongle named the temple.

According to legend, Heavenward Temple is the dividing line between the immortal and mortal worlds. During ancient times, those who paid respect to Emperor Zhenwu would think that they had entered the Heaven, and they worshiped here and then continued hiking up the mountain.

The statues of the Jade Emperor and Emperor Zhenwu are enshrined in Heavenward Temple. At present, the decrees and inscriptions to Wudang Mountain written by emperors of different dynasties exhibited here tell us how Wudang Mountain reached its peak with the support of the emperors and imperial families.

Sun Biyun（孙碧云）, a famous Taoist monk, was once in charge of the temple. He enjoyed such a high status in Taoism that Emperor Zhu Yuanzhang once granted him an interview. Emperor Zhu Di also asked him to design the construction on Wudang Mountain. After thinking hard, it was Sun Biyun who combined the legend of Emperor Zhenwu with the buildings on Wudang Mountain.

Walking out of the temple, we can see a stone stele "Wan Fang Duo Nan Ci Deng Lin（万方多难此登临）" made by Guo Dejie（郭德杰）, the wife of Li Zongren（李宗仁）, a famous anti-Japanese hero. This sentence was written by Du Fu（杜甫）, a famous poet in the Tang Dynasty. Guo used this sentence to describe how she felt during the period of Anti-Japanese War. Another stele made by the people from Guangxi Province was set up for Li Zongren. It records Li Zongren succeeded in wiping out 20,000 Japanese soldiers.

5.4 First, Second, and Third Celestial Gates and the Pilgrimage Gate

First Celestial Gate, Second Celestial Gate, Third Celestial Gate and the Pilgrimage Gate were built in 1412 and a necessary road to the Golden Hall before the Qing Dynasty (1644-1911). The characters on the gate were written by Mu Xin, one of Zhu Di's sons-in-law.

5.5 Wenchang Hall

This is Wenchang Hall. Wenchang is a Taoist deity in Chinese mythology, known as the Emperor of Culture and Literature（掌管士人功名禄位之神）. A lot of Chinese people pray to Wenchang for good exam scores. In 374, Zhang Yu（张育）, Sichuan Province, raised a rebellion and fought to death; people built a temple for him. What's more, he was also regarded as a filial exemplar; he cut his flesh to cook for his sick mother. During the Yuan and Ming Dynasties, he received more and more respect and sacrifices from worshipers, especially from those who wanted to pass imperial exams. February 3rd of the lunar calendar is regarded as his birthday. Now those who wish for a promotion will come to Wenchang Temple with flowers, fruits and desserts. Parents who have naughty children may also come here with green Chinese onion (Cong, whose pronunciation is similar to cleverness), celery (Qincai, whose pronunciation is similar to diligence) and Zongzi with mince in it (Zongzi, whose pronunciation is similar to be No. one in the exam).

5.6 Immortal-Meeting Bridge

Beside the temple is Star-Picking Bridge（摘星桥）. It is also called Immortal-Meeting Bridge （会仙桥）. It was made in the Ming Dynasty. It is 13.7 meters long and 4.7 meters wide. It is said that when Zhenwu flew to Heaven, the Jade Emperor sent God Ziwei, his master, to meet Zhenwu here.

VI. The Palace of Supreme Harmony

6.1 Introduction

The Palace of Supreme Harmony lies on top of Tianzhu Peak, the highest hill of Wudang Mountain. Since the 17th century (the Qing Dynasty), it has been called "the Palace of Supreme Harmony". Since 1956, it has been listed as Provincial Key Cultural Relics Protecting Unit. Since 1961, it has been listed as National Key Cultural Relics Protecting Unit by the State Council. Since 1984, it has been open to the public as a religious site. It's a must-see sight for each visitor. Several years ago, a photographer took a photo of the mountain from the sky. Can you imagine what it looks like? The whole mountain looks as if a snake is inter-twined with a tortoise.

600 years ago, Zhu Di, the fourth emperor of the Ming Dynasty, ordered the construction of the palace. 4 years later, the construction was completed. He also named it Mountain of Supreme Harmony (太和山); Wudang Mountain became more important than the Five Sacred Mountains (五岳) in China. During the reign of Emperor Jiajing, the Palace of Supreme Harmony was enlarged to more than 520 rooms.

6.2 Inscriptions of Yi Zhu Qing Tian

On the rock, we can see four Chinese characters "Yi Zhu Qing Tian"（一柱擎天）, which mean Tianzhu Peak is so high that it looks like a pillar propping up the sky. They were written by Zong Yi（宗彝）, a calligrapher, also head of the Education Department during the Republic of China (1912-1949). Zong yi happens to be one of the twelve Chinese symbols of sovereignty（十二章纹）appeared on the sacrificial robes of the Son of Heaven. They are sun, moon, stars, mountains, dragon, pheasant, Zong yi, waterweed, grain, fire, axe and fu. The sun, the moon and the stars show emperors pour out his blessings upon his people. Mountains are symbols of stability and the earth. Dragon symbolizes the emperors who could rule the nation skillfully. Pheasant is a symbol of literary refinement. Zong yi is a pair of bronze sacrificial cups, symbolizing respect for one's parents. One cup has a tiger (physical strength), the other a monkey (cleverness). Waterweed represents purity. Grain represents the country's capacity to feed its people. Fire represents intellectual brilliance. Axe represents the power to punish. Fu represents the power to judge. (Adapted from http://www.powerhousemuseum.com/hsc/evrev/chinese_dress.htm)

This poem was made by Li Pinxian（李品仙）, who worked together with Li Zongren in the Anti-Japanese War, killing more than 20,000 Japanese invaders.

In 1939, Li Zongren also wrote "Zheng Jun Jing Wu（整军经武）", which mean that Chinese soldiers should be disciplined so that they can be strong and brave enough to fight against Japanese enemies.

6.3 Pilgrimage Hall

This hall was built in 1412. During the Ming Dynasty, ordinary pilgrims were forbidden to the Golden Hall; they were only allowed to pay their respect to Emperor Zhenwu in Pilgrimage Hall.

There is a plaque with four Chinese characters, San Jiao Zu Shi （三教祖师）, which mean that Emperor Zhenwu was respected in Buddhism, Taoism and Confucianism. Emperor Zhu Di raised a rebellion and seized the throne. In order to make his enthronement lawful, he claimed that his power was granted by Emperor Zhenwu. Besides that, he also put the status of Taoism ahead of the other religions.

In front of the hall stands a pavilion without walls. On the two sides of the hall are the Bell Tower and Drum Tower, in which is a big bronze clock made in 1415. The bronze clock, 1.57 meters high and 1.435 meters wide, is the largest on Wudang Mountain.

Here we can see two bronze-cast tablets. The right one weighs 9 tons. The imperial tablet was made when Emperor Jiajing ordered to start a large scale construction on Wudang Mountain in 1552. We can see two projecting Chinese characters "Yu Zhi （御制）", which mean "made by the emperor order" and the following characters are sunken. Projecting characters stand for Yang and sunken characters stand for Yin. Here Yin and Yang are balanced. The other one was made in 1560, recording the events on Wudang Mountain.

Inside the hall, Emperor Zhenwu, Jade Girl, Golden Boy and eight other attendants are honored, some of which were carved in the Ming Dynasty and some in the Qing Dynasty.

6.4 Forbidden Wall

Now we have come to Nan Tian Men (Southern Celestial Gate). According to Chinese legend, Southern Celestial Gate is the most important gate to get into Heaven. There are three doorways in Southern Celestial Gate: the holy gate, the ghost gate, and the human gate. The ghost gate is a symbolic one, which has been closed since it was built because there is no permission for the evil ghosts to appear in such a holy land. The holy gate was not open until the ministers sent by emperors visited this place, but the human gate is always open for the pilgrims to pay homage to Emperor Zhenwu.

Do you know why the wall was built? In 1416, people constructed the Golden Hall on Tianzhu Peak. But there were no walls around the hall at that time. In 1419, Zhu Di ordered to build Forbidden Wall on Tianzhu Peak to collect Qi and demanded that the construction of the wall follow the rise and fall of the mountain, with no change of the shape of the mountain and that the wall be strong and steady. In Forbidden Wall there are four stone-carved gates in four directions, but only Southern Celestial Gate is accessible.

The construction lasted five years. The wall is 344 meters long. The base is 2.4 meters wide and the top is 1.26 meters wide; the wall looks like a pyramid without a top.

6.5 Inscriptions of Fang Zhenwu's Poem

The poem was made by Fang Zhenwu（方振武）, a Chinese military officer in the early twentieth century. He was active in fighting against the Japanese invaders, so he was rejected by Chiang Kai-shek（蒋介石）, who detained and removed him from office in October 1929. In this case, he went to Wudang Mountain and wrote the poem, expressing his strong sense of patriotism.

6.6 Lingguan Hall

This is Lingguan Hall（灵官殿）for Wang Shan（王善）, head of 500 guardian deities（500 灵官）. According to legend, those who are not filial to parents, or do bad deeds will be frightened to death when passing the place, for Wang Shan said, "How dare you come to such a holy land if you are an evildoer?" Wang Shan, in Taoism, is a guardian deity at the mountain gates. Similar to Bodhisattva Wei Tuo（韦驮）, his main duty is to overlook the altars, protect the laws, settle the disputes of immortals and punish the disloyalty. Do you know Bodhisattva Wei Tuo? If not, I guess you are familiar with a kind of flower which bears large, strongly fragrant flowers that bloom at nights for a short period of time. There is a love story between the flower and Wei Tuo.

Legend has it that Tan Hua（昙花）, a flower goddess, blooms every day and falls in love with the young gardener. When the Jade Emperor learns it, he commands that the flower goddess be allowed to bloom just at nights for a short time and the young gardener be sent to be a Buddhist monk, named Wei Tuo. Many years have passed; Wei Tuo empties his mind and forgets the flower goddess. On the contrary, knowing that he comes to her to collect morning dews in late springs, the flower goddess gathers all her essence to display her best when seeing Wei Tuo. Unfortunately, Wei Tuo can't recognize her. Hundreds of years later, a man asks the flower goddess why she looks sad. Surprised at the fact that how a common man can see her, the flower goddess answers that it is beyond his ability to help her. Then she keeps silent. Forty years later, the man asks the same question and the flower goddess repeats the answer. Another forty years later, the man, very old now, raises the question for a third time. The flower goddess tells him the truth and the old man says he is the very gardener who weeds and waters her. After finishing his words, he holds the flower and enters nirvana. In Heaven, they meet each other and realize their dream.

Here we can see six tablets issued by five emperors of the Ming Dynasty. You may wonder why? Let me tell you the story. There are 16 emperors of the Ming Dynasty. (1)The first tablet was issued by Zhu Gaozhi（朱高炽）, Zhu Di's eldest son. When he took the throne, he issued the imperial edict and sent a minister to Wudang Mountain to pay homage to Emperor Zhenwu. He was on the throne for only nine months. (2) The second one was issued by Zhu Zhanji（朱瞻基）, Zhu Gaozhi's eldest son. Zhu Di liked him very much. Zhu Di handed over his power to Zhu Gaozhi just for the sake of Zhu Zhanji. He also issued the imperial edict and sent a minister to Wudang Mounatins as his father. He was on the throne for 11 years. (3) The third and fifth one were both issued by Zhu Qizhen （朱祁镇）, Zhu Zhanji's eldest son, as he mounted to the throne twice. He first came to the throne at the age of 9, so he relied heavily on his eunuch Wang Zhen（王振）, who advised Zhu Qizhen declare a war against the northern ethnic group—the Mongol. Unluckily, he was captured and imprisoned by the Mongols. In order to calm the crisis at home, his brother Zhu Qiyu（朱祁钰）was installed as Emperor. Zhu Qizhen was released one year later in 1450 but when he returned to Beijing, he was immediately put under house arrest by his brother for almost seven years. He resided in the southern hall of the Forbidden City and all outside contacts were severely curtailed by Zhu Qiyu. Zhu Qizhen's son (later Emperor Chenghua) was stripped of the title of crown prince and replaced by Zhu Qiyu's own son, who died shortly after. Overcome with grief, Zhu Qiyu fell ill and Zhu Qizhen decided to depose Zhu Qiyu by a palace coup. After the coup, Zhu Qizhen went on to rule for another seven years. He came to the throne twice, so he sent ministers to Wudang Mountain twice. The fourth one was issued by Zhu Qiyu. (4) The sixth one was issued by Zhu Jianshen （朱见深）. He was Zhu Qizhen's son. He was only two years old when his father was captured by the Mongols and held captive in 1449. Even after being set free by the Mongols, his father was put under house arrest for almost seven years by his uncle, the Jingtai Emperor（景泰帝，朱祁钰）. During this time, Lady Wan, a palace girl, who was 19 years older than he, took care of him. When he ascended to the throne at the age of 16, she quickly became his favorite consort. She gave birth to a child in 1464, but the baby died shortly after.

From then on, she prevented the young emperor from bearing any offspring. Lady Wan and her eunuchs would either induce abortion to those who were about to bear the emperor's child or administer poison to the mother and child if birth had occurred. It was not until 1475 that Emperor Zhu Jianshen discovered that he had a son who survived and was raised in secrecy. During the early period of his administration, he carried out new government policies to reduce tax and strengthen the dynasty. However, these did not last and by the closing years of his reign, governmental affairs once again fell into the hands of eunuchs. Peasant uprisings occurred throughout the country. His reign was also more autocratic than his predecessors'; he set up a spy agency, punishing those whom they suspected of treason.

There is a horizontal board inscribed "圣恩普沛". It means "May the blessings of Emperor Zhenwu be upon all people." There is a couplet:"天知地知未不知，善报恶报终有报." It means bad deeds, as well as good, may come back to the doers.

6.7 Golden Hall

This is Golden Hall. Do you know how many ancient golden halls still exist in China? There are six: two on Wudang Mountain, one on Mingfeng Mountain（鸣凤山）, one in the Summer Palace（颐和园）, one in Suzhou and one on Wutai Mountain（五台山）. It is the second biggest existing gilded copper (alloy) hall in China; it weighs 90 tons and it is 5.45 meters high, 4.4 meters wide and 3.15 meters deep. The biggest one is on the top of Mingfeng Mountain, Kunming, Yunnan Province; it weighs 250 tons and it is 6.7 meters high and 6.2

meters wide and deep. They are called golden halls because copper and gold were interchangeable in ancient China.

The hall demonstrated a high level of casting technology in the 15th century. Emperor Zhu Di attached great importance to the construction of the hall; all the parts were cast in Beijing and the transportation was arranged by the emperor. They moved along the Great Canal（大运河）by boat to Nanjing and then along the Changjiang River and its tributary—Hanjiang River to the foot of Wudang Mountain, then 100,000 workers carried the parts up to Tianzhu Peak, put them together and painted it with gold mud—a mixture of mercury and gold. At last, it was baked over the charcoal fire so that mercury evaporates and pure gold remains. How was gold mud made? First, heat the mercury, strike the gold into gold pieces, and then put the gold pieces into the mercury. Finally, stir and heat the mixture until it turns into gold mud.

Inside the hall is a lamp. It is said that the lamp has been burning for about 600 years. There are two reasons. The first one is that the hall faces east, so it prevents the wind from the north in winter and the wind from the south in summer. The second one is that the hall was built with no openings, so the wind can find no way to enter it.

Look up, and we can see the four characters "Jin Guang Miao Xiang"（金光妙相）. They were written by Emperor Kangxi. It means that Emperor Zhenwu beams with honor and distinction. In 1673, Emperor Kangxi sent some attendants to Wudang Mountain to worship Emperor Zhenwu. They were also ordered to draw a picture of the whole Wudang Mountain. Why? On the one hand, Emperor

Kangxi could appreciate the mountain. On the other hand, he wanted to make military preparation for a war. Wu Sangui（吴三桂）, a governor in Yunnan, posed a great threat to the government. What's more, he also built a golden hall on the top of Mingfeng Mountain in Yunnan, so Emperor Kangxi was determined to take back his power. As expected, in 1674, Wu Sangui's subordinates rebelled on Wudang Mountain. Because of the full preparation, the Qing government defeated them. After eight years' fight, (in 1681) Emperor Kangxi succeeded in putting down the rebellions and consolidated his power. In order to show his gratitude for Emperor Zhenwu, he wrote five plaques and had them sent to Wudang Mountain. Jin Guang Miao Xiang is one of them.

In the middle is the statue of Emperor Zhenwu. He is half-closed. Do you know why his eyes are not wide open or closed? When nourishing energy, closing your eyes may lead to sleepiness and opening your eyes may distract your attention.

There is also a snake-tortoise figure. Both snake and tortoise represent longevity, which also shows what Taoists pursue. Snake stands for Yin, and tortoise stands for Yang. This means that Yin and Yang should be balanced.

Let's look at the roof. The flying eaves are decorated by a man riding a bird and five mythical animals—dragon, phoenix, lion（狮）, heavenly horse（天马）, and auspicious seahorse（海马）. The roof shows that it has the highest status on Wudang Mountain.

Let's look at the base. According to experts, the base is made of fossils, which formed about 500 million years ago. It's rare to build a hall on the fossils in the world.

Now you can count the number of the bars. There are 148 bars. They were donated by the pilgrims from Yunnan Province 400 years ago. Here we can still see their names and addresses.

Can you see something yellow? This is genuine gold. The gold mud is made according to an appropriate proportion between mercury and gold, so some gold is left and installed here.

One of the most unique features about the Golden Hall is that it's conductive. Whenever there is thunder and lightning, the fire ball moves around the Golden Hall without damaging it. As a result, having existed for more than 600 years, the Golden Hall is still kept intact and stands here with luster. But in 1964, in order to protect the hall, it was equipped with a lightening rod. Since then, the scene "a fire ball moving around the hall" has never been seen.

In front of the Golden Hall, though the two bronze pavilions were built during the Jiajing reign (1521-1566) of the Ming Dynasty, they are still intact. One houses a bell and the other houses a chime.

On both sides of the hall, there are rooms for drawing lots and deity seals.

At the back of the hall is the Parent Hall housing statues of Emperor Zhenwu's parents.

Extended Reading 8: Imperial Roof Decoration

Chinese imperial roof decoration was only allowed on official buildings of the empire.

At the head of the procession will be a man riding a phoenix, one legend suggests that this represents an emperor who grew greedy for power and was hanged for treason.

In between will be mythical beasts, usually an odd number of them. The mythical beasts are set to pounce upon the man and devour him should he stray from performing his duties with faithfulness and rectitude.

The maximum number of beasts is nine, including dragon, phoenix, lion, heavenly horse（天马）, auspicious seahorse（海马）, mythical lion（狻猊）, wind-and storm-summoning fish（狎鱼）, courageous goat-bull（獬豸）, and evil-dispelling bull（斗牛）. The Hall of Supreme Harmony in Palace Museum, however, is an exception. It has a man riding a phoenix and ten beasts, with the last one called Hangshi（行什）, which means "ranked tenth"; this hall enjoys the highest status in China. What are they used for? Only for decorative purpose? According to architects, these strange-looking creatures can prevent the roof from sliding. Moreover, the number and the size of the creatures on the eaves indicate the importance of the building.

6.8 Fate-Turning Hall（Zhuanyun Hall）

Look at the bronze hall, which was made in 1307 in Wuchang and was the earliest preserved bronze hall in China. The bronze hall was formerly placed on the top of Tianzhu Peak during the Yuan Dynasty. When Zhu Di became emperor, he wanted to build a bigger bronze hall to demonstrate his royal dignity. So another hall was erected in the Ming Dynasty, and the bronze hall was transported here and protected by another brick hall.

Since it was transported from one place to another place, it was also called Zhuanyun Hall（转运殿）. In Chinese, Zhuanyun means "transporting"; it also reminds people of "having a change of luck" or "turning for a better fate". Many visitors like to walk between the bronze hall and the brick hall in hopes of having better luck and a brighter future.

The bronze hall is 2.44 meters in height and 2.165 meters in width and length. Here we can see many inscriptions, recording the names and addresses of the donators and fundraisers. Look up, and we can see the symbols of Three Pure Ones (the three highest gods in Taoism), six stars in the Small Dipper（南斗六星）and seven stars in the Big Dipper（北斗七星）. With a mortise-and-tenon structure, fine craftwork, rich styles and dignified sculpture, it is an important artifact to study and research the buildings of Wudang Mountain built in the Yuan Dynasty.

6.9. The Scripture Hall

The scripture Hall was first built during the reign of Emperor Yongle in the Ming Dynasty（1403-1425）and rebuilt in the 29th year of Emperor Daoguang in the Qing Dynasty (1850). Scripture Hall is a place for Taoists to read scriptures and to attend the service. Taoists read scriptures for one hour in the morning and one hour at dusk every day in hope of purifying their souls and prolonging their life.

Now we can see a plaque with four Chinese characters "Bai Yu Jing Zhong"（白玉京中）. "Bai Yu" are black and stand for Yang. "Jing Zhong" are yellow and stand for Yin. It shows that Yin and

Yang should be balanced. In Taoism, "Bai Yu Jing" refers to the residence for Heavenly Emperor. So it means the Scripture Hall is a holy place for Heavenly Emperor to have an audience with the immortals.

"金阙绕红云现十七光而道观仙佛，玉京凝紫气历三千劫而位极人天." "金阙" and "玉京" both refer to the place where Heavenly Emperor lives. Most of the Taoist monks on Wudang Mountain can attain wisdom after experiencing a lot of failure, including Emperor Zhenwu, who was greatly respected in the world. If you stick to what you believe in, your chance of success will be increased.

Inside the hall, we can see a plaque "法开元武". It means that the way to the Tao was found by Emperor Xuanwu. The hall is also a place for the immortals to get together; when entering the door to the Tao, you will have the opportunity to discuss the Tao with other immortals.

Opposite the plaque, we can see another plaque "Sheng Tian Li Di"（生天立地）. They were written by Emperor Daoguang in the Qing Dynasty. In the Golden Hall, there is another plaque written by Emperor Kangxi in the Qing Dynasty. We can see the Qing government also showed great concern for Taoism. Sheng Tian Li Di implies that Emperor Daoguang hoped that he was as capable as Emperor Zhenwu; all the subjects were loyal and well-behaved. During the reign of Emperor Daoguang, China experienced major problems with opium, which was imported into China by British merchants. He issued many edicts against opium in the 1820s and 1830s, which were carried out by Commissioner Lin Zexu（林则徐）.

Lin Zexu's effort to halt the spread of opium in China led directly to the First Opium War.

In the middle of the shrine is the statue of Yuanshi Tianzun（元始天尊）, one of the three highest Gods in the Taoist pantheon. It is believed that Yuanshi Tianzun came to being at the beginning of the universe and then created Heaven and Earth. From him all things arose.

Above it is the statue of Goddess Doumu（斗姆）with three eyes, four faces and eight arms. The four faces represent four symbols: Azure dragon, white tiger, vermilion bird and black tortoise. In her hands are the sun, the moon, a bell, an arrow and other instruments. She enjoys a high status among the deities in religious Taoism. In Chinese, "斗" means the Bigger Dipper, and "姆" means mother; "斗姆" means mother of many stars, so it is respected.

Below the statue of Yuanshi Tianzun, we can see five statues. In the middle is the statue of the Jade Emperor. Although the Jade Emperor does not enjoy the highest status, he is the most powerful. He is the supreme administrator of Heaven and Earth; everything is under his control. Another one is the statue of Emperor Zhenwu and the other three are the statues of Official Heaven（天官）, Official Earth（地官）and Official Water（水官）. Why? In ancient times, Heaven, earth and water were regarded the most important elements in their lives. Official Heaven is believed to bring happiness to people, Official Earth forgives sins and Official Water can free people from troubles. They keep track of good and bad deeds and they are considered to be deeply compassionate towards all living things.

There is a couplet: 东土圣人曾向吾门求至道，西方佛子还与我国悟真空. "东土" means China, "圣人" means Confucius (Confucius, Lao Tzu and Sakyamuni are regarded as the three sages in the east). It means that Confucius once asked Lao Tzu for Tao (the laws of the nature); Buddhist monks also consulted Taoist monks about the natural law in the universe. There is a story between Confucius and Lao Tzu in extremely old age. Lao Tzu asked Confucius what he saw in his mouth. Confucius said he saw nothing. Lao Tzu asked, "No teeth?" Confucius replied, "No teeth. But I do see a tongue." Lao Tzu wanted to demonstrate the fact that those hard and brittle things disappear; the soft and yieldings things remain. Lu Xun, a famous Chinese writer, believes the root of Chinese culture lies in Taoism.

Can you see a plaque with four Chinese characters: Huang Liang Meng Jue（黄粱梦觉）? Huang Liang is a kind of rice, Meng means dream and Jue means over; this idiom means "the dream is over before the rice is ready; the dream is sweet but temporary." There is a legend: A person had failed the imperial exams many times. Now he was hungry and came to a pub in Han Dan（邯郸）of Hebei Province. Lv Dongbin cooked for him. Before the rice was ready, he dreamed that he passed the imperial exam and became an official. But at the age of 80, he was seriously ill and dying. At this moment, he woke up, seeing no changes had taken place. It occurred to him that fame and wealth were nothing. So he decided to travel around the world and purify his soul.

Here is the statue of Goddess of Mercy（观音菩萨）. Taoists believe that Taoism, Confucianism and Buddhism should be synergetic; Goddess of Mercy in Buddhism is also worshiped here and revered as Cihang Daoren.

Walk out of the hall, and we can see eight murals, telling us the process how Zhenwu refined himself on Wudang Mountain.

6.10 Cableway

Here we can see five Chinese characters: Wu Dang Shan Suo Dao（武当山索道）. They were written by Liu Binsen（刘炳森）, a famous modern calligrapher. This is the place to take a cable car. From August 1997 to 2010, people could go to the Golden Hall by cable car, but it took 25 minutes to cover the distance and each car could carry only 2 persons. Since 2010, the equipments from Austria have been used; now only 5 minutes is needed and each car may carry 8 persons. It can transport 1,500 people an hour in a single track.

6.11 Qiongtai Temple

This is Qiongtai Temple. It was said that Zhenwu refined himself in Taizipo Palace, flew to Heaven in Nanyan Palace, and was appointed as Emperor of the North Pole in Qiongtai Temple（在琼台授封）. So Wudang Taoists show great respect for Qiongtai Temple.

Qiongtai Temple lies 2.5 kilometers southeast of Tianzhu Peak and the direct distance is 1,350 meters between Qiongtai Temple and Tianzhu Peak.

It was first built in the Yuan Dynasty and expanded in the Ming and Qing Dynasties. Qiongtai Temple has three temples: the Upper

Temple （上观）, the Middle Temple （中观）, and the Lower Temple （下观）. Unfortunately, the three temples were greatly damaged in a war in 1856. Now the Upper Temple covers an area of 3,600 square meters. Here we can only see a stone statue of Zhenwu and steles of the Ming Dynasty. In the Lower Temple, with an area of 571 square meters, there are 13 rooms including the main hall and side houses. The best preserved among the three temples is the Middle Temple with an area of 479 square meters. Now we can see a stone hall of the Yuan Dynasty. The stone hall, facing east, sits on the right side of the main hall. It covers an area of 18 square meters. Inside the hall are many statues, among which a bronze-cast gilded statue of Zhenwu of the Ming Dynasty is very precious. Besides, the biggest stone statue of Zhenwu is also kept here.

6.12 Eight-Immortal Temple

Now we have come to Eight-Immortal Temple. How did the temple get its name? It is said that eight immortals planned to the Golden Hall to worship Emperor Zhenwu. When they came here, they were attracted by the tea here and decided to settle down. Let me tell you the legends about the Eight Immortals.

1) Tieguai Li （铁拐李, meaning Li with an Iron Crutch）was a Taoist by the name of Li Xuan who received his Enlightenment from Lao Tzu. Once his soul left his body to travel around but had to enter the corpse of a starved beggar when he found his own body mistakenly burnt by his disciple. He then had an earthly form with unkempt hair, a dirty face, a bare abdomen and a crippled leg. He

used an iron cane or crutch, hence his popular name.

2) Han Zhongli（汉钟离）was also called Zhong Liquan. A strong light came into the room before he came into the world. When he grew up, he became a general. Once he was defeated in a battle and got lost. At this time, he came across an immortal, who told him the secrets of alchemy and immortality.

3) Zhang Guolao（张果老）was a hermit in the Zhongtiao Mountains（中条山）for a long time. He is said to have already been several hundred years old in the reign of Empress Wu Zetian (690-705). Summoned by the Empress, he feigned death by magic in order to avoid meeting her. He used to travel on a white donkey which could cover thousands of miles in a single day. When taking a rest, he would fold up the donkey as if it were made of paper and put it into his suitcase. He is usually depicted riding backward on his donkey, which is, facing the tail of the donkey.

4) He Xiangu（何仙姑）was a Tang Dynasty girl of Guangdong Province. At the age of 14, she had a dream that some immortals told her to take some mica powder. Do as what she was told, and she became an immortal. After that, she was so agile that her body could float from one peak to another collecting fruit for her mother. Another source says that she was a Taoist nun during the Song Dynasty, famous as a fortune-teller.

5) Lan Caihe（蓝采和）, according to some sources, was usually dressed in blue tatters, with one foot bare and the other in a boot, wandering through the country, begging along the thoroughfares and singing drunkenly to the cadence of castanets. One day in an inn,

music of flutes and mouth-organs was heard descending from the sky. Lan was suddenly wafted off into the air and vanished.

6) Lv Dingbin（吕洞宾）was a native of Shaanxi (some say, of Shanxi) Province and lived during the Tang Dynasty. Failing the imperial examinations twice, he led a vagrant life for years. At the age of sixty-four, he met Han Zhongli in an inn, who taught him the secrets of alchemy. Then he became a hermit in the Zhongnan Mountains to seek the Way of Immortality.

7) Han Xiangzi（韩湘子）, intelligent and unrestrained in nature, is said to be a distant nephew of the great Tang poet-thinker Han Yu, who told Han Xiangzi to bury himself in study. Instead of working hard, Han Xiangzi bullied his classmates. In order to prove his ability, he managed, once in a winter, to make rose-peonies blossom in a few days in different colors, which astonished his uncle.

8) Cao Guojiu（曹国舅）is said to have lived during the Song Dynasty and his name was Cao Yi（曹佾）, Guojiu being a semi-official title for the brothers of the empress. He had a brother who, taking advantage of his imperial connection, became a notorious evildoer. Ashamed of his brother and afraid of becoming implicated, he scattered his wealth among the poor and went into the mountains to seek the Way of Enlightenment.

Their images appear in all sorts of arts and crafts, including furniture, porcelain, paintings and embroideries, often to convey the idea of a leisurely, carefree life. The best known tale that involves all of them together is Ba Xian Guo Hai or The Eight Immortals Crossing the Sea（八仙过海）. This has given rise to an everyday saying, "people are said to be emulating the example of the Eight Immortals crossing the sea when trying to accomplish the same task using different methods."

VII. Shopping Center

The shopping center (the Silver Street) was completed in 2008 and the opposite one (the Golden Street) was completed in 2006. Here we can buy souvenirs for ourselves, relatives and friends.

7.1 Wudang Sword

Wudang Mountain is the birthplace of Wudang Boxing and Wudang Sword. Practicing Wudang sword can help promote the health. Wudang Sword is one of the four weapons in the world of martial arts; many tourists give first priority to Wudang Sword.

7.2 Wudang Tea

The tea produced here is a kind of green tea. With no fermentation, green tea is the most natural of all Chinese tea classes. About 70% of China's teas are green tea.

Chinese tea may be classified into five categories according to the different methods by which it is processed. 1) Green tea is the variety which keeps the original color of the tea leaves without fermentation during processing. 2) Black tea, known as "red tea" (hong cha) in China, is the category which is fermented before baking; it is a later variety developed on the basis of the green tea. 3) Oolong tea represents a variety half way between the green and the black teas, being made after partial fermentation. 4) Compressed tea is a kind of tea which is compressed and hardened into a certain shape. It is good for transport and storage and is mainly supplied to the ethnic minorities living in the border areas of the country. As compressed tea is black in color in its commercial form, so it is also known in China as "black tea". Most of the compressed tea is in the form of bricks; it is, therefore, generally called "brick tea", though it is sometimes also in the form of cakes and bowls. 5) Scented tea is made by mixing fragrant flowers in the tea leaves in the course of processing. The flowers commonly used for this purpose are jasmine and magnolia among others. Jasmine tea is a well-known favorite with the northerners of China and with a growing number of foreigners.

In China, people think different teas prefer different tea wares. Green tea prefers glass tea ware, scented tea porcelain ware while Oolong tea performs best in purple clay tea ware.

Drinking green tea offers numerous benefits. Green tea can reduce the risk of cardiovascular disease, radiation-related injuries, dental cavities, eye problems and cancer. It can also help lose weight, refresh the mind, clear heat within the human body, stop chapped skin, get rid of foot odor and bad breath, lighten black ring if we put gauze with tea on the eyes, and make your hair soft, shiny and smooth if we wash hair with tea water.

As you add a cup of tea to your daily routine, please check the following tips which help you reap the maximum health benefits. 1)

Drink it hot. Tea oxidizes quickly after brewing, and its nutrients diminish overtime. It is suggested that you drink it hot to get the best out of tea. 2) Do not drink too much strong tea. It is likely to upset your stomach and cause insomnia if you make the tea too strong. 3) The best time to drink is in between meals. Do not drink tea soon after or before meals. Otherwise it may quench appetite when your stomach is empty, or cause indigestion when your stomach is full. 4) Do not drink with medication. Tea contains large amount of Tannin, which will react with certain elements in the medicine, thus reduce medical effects. You can drink tea a couple of hours after you take medicine. 5) Green tea is the best option for office workers. Green tea helps prevent computer radiation and supplement moisture content of the human body. 6) Don't steep green tea in too hot water or for too long. The biggest mistake you can make with green tea is to steep it in water that's too hot. Green tea is different from black tea in that it needs water that's only about 176°F to 185°F (80 °C to 85 °C). The second biggest mistake is to steep it for too long. Green tea shouldn't be steeped for more than 2 to 2.5 minutes.

In China, there are customs about tea. Tea is always offered immediately to a guest in Chinese home. Besides, the tea is injected into a teacup only seven tenth, and it is said that the other three tenth is filled with friendship and affection. If a person's cup is filled, that person may knock their bent index and middle fingers on the table to express gratitude to the person who served the tea. This custom is said to have originated in the Qing Dynasty when Emperor Qianlong would travel in disguise through the empire. Servants were told not to reveal their master's identity. One day in a restaurant, the emperor, after pouring himself a cup of tea, filled a servant's cup as well. To that servant it was a huge honor. Out of reflex he wanted to kneel and express his thanks. He could not kneel and kowtow to the emperor since that would reveal the emperor's identity, so he bent his fingers on the table to express his gratitude and respect to the emperor. The bent fingers for knocking are technically supposed to signify a bowing servant. It should be noted that in formal tea ceremonies nodding of the head and/or saying "thank you" is more appropriate.

Thanks to the abundant rainfall and mild and moist climate, the tea produced here is of high quality. Most of high-quality tea leaves are produced in thirty degrees north latitude, so remember to take some for your families and friends.

Extended Reading 9: Chinese Tea

Tea drinking has long been an important part of Chinese culture. A Chinese saying identifies the seven basic daily necessities as fuel, rice, oil, salt, soy sauce, vinegar, and tea.

According to Chinese legend, tea was discovered accidentally by the Chinese Emperor Shen Nong in 2737 B.C. On one summer day, Emperor Shen Nong and his servants were tired and thirsty after walking a long distance; they rested under a tree and boiled water. A few leaves fell into the pot. The emperor was interested in the new liquid because it had a pleasant smell, so he drank the infusion and found it delicious and refreshing. From then on, people began to drink tea.

Another legend is that Shen Nong tasted different kinds of plants to make sure what could be used as food and what could be used as medicine. One day, he was poisoned after tasting one plant and lay down under a tea tree. The water from the tree fell into his mouth and moved around the body as if it was checking something. Then Shen Nong came back to life. From then on, he named the plant "cha". In Chinese, "check" has the similar pronunciation with "tea".

Tea was used as offerings in the Western Zhou, vegetables in the Spring and Autumn Period, and medicine in the Warring Period. Later in the Western Han Dynasty, it became a main commodity. During 300 years between the Three Kingdoms Period and the Northern and Southern Dynasties, especially the latter, Buddhism was popular and Buddhists applied tea to relieve sleep during meditation hours, so tea trees spread along valleys around temples. That is why people say tea and Buddhism accompanied each other in their development. In the Tang Dynasty, a scholar named Lu Yu published the first definitive book, *The Tea Classics* （《茶经》）, on tea after he spent over twenty years studying the subject. This book included his knowledge of planting, processing, tasting, and brewing tea. Tea became popular among ordinary people. Later, a Song Dynasty emperor helped the spread of tea consumption further by indulging in this wonderful custom. He enjoyed tea drinking so much that he bestowed tea as gifts only to those who were worthy. In the Ming Dynasty, tea trade began to play an important role in the government economy; the "Tea and Horse Bureau" was set up to supervise the tea trade.

In the 6th century, a Buddhist monk introduced tea to Japan where the Japanese Tea Ceremony was created. In Japan, tea was elevated to an art form which requires years of dedicated studying. Unlike the Japanese, the Chinese tend to view tea drinking as a form of enjoyment: to have tea after a meal or to serve tea when guests visit.

Tea was introduced to Europe in the 1600s; it was introduced to England in 1669. At that time, the drink was enjoyed only by the aristocracy because a pound of tea cost an average British laborer the equivalent of nine months in wages. The British began to import tea in larger qualities to satisfy the rapidly expanding market. Tea became Britain's most important item of trade from China. All classes were able to drink tea as the tea trade increased and became less of a luxury. Now, tea is low in price and readily available.

Today, there are more than 1,500 types of teas to choose from because over 25 countries cultivate tea as a plantation crop. China is one of the main producers of tea, and tea remains China's national drink. (Adapted from http://www.beijingtrip.com/feature/tea.htm)

7.3 Turquoise

Let me tell you a legend. A fight for power broke out between Zhuan Xu(颛顼), the descendant of Huang Di (Yellow Emperor) and Gong Gong(共工), who was stronger, but less wiser than Zhuan Xu. Gong Gong was defeated by Zhuan Xu. Angry from embarrassment, he crashed into Buzhou Mountain(不周山), the sky-supporting pillar. With the collapse of the pillar, everything was in disorder. Nv Wa

（女娲）, goddess of creation in Chinese ancient myth, had to mend the sky with stones of different colors, among which was turquoise here.

As to the discovery of the stone, there is also a famous story. The stone was formerly called He Shi Bi（和氏璧, The Jade Disc of He）. He Shi means Surname He, referring to Bian He（卞和）. Bian He found a piece of jade stone in the Chu Kingdom. He recognized the value of the jade inside the stone and offered it to King Li（厉王）. King Li had his jeweler examine the stone, who said it was just an ordinary stone. King Li punished him by having his left foot cut off. As King Li passed away and his son, Wu, came to the throne. Bian He once again offered his grand stone to the King. Wu had his jeweler examine the stone, who also said it was nothing but a stone. King Wu（武王）then punished him by having his right foot cut off. As King Wu passed away and his son, Wen, came to the throne. Bian He held his jade stone and cried for three days and nights. As he ran out of tears, blood came down his cheeks. King Wen（文王）sent his man to ask him, "Are you grieving for your feet?" He replied, "I'm not grieving for my feet. I'm grieving for the wrongs that a precious jade is called a stone, and an honest man, a liar." Upon hearing that, King Wen had his jeweler cut open the stone. A large pure jade was seen nestling inside the stone. King Wen named the jade He Shi in honor of Bian He. This is turquoise. From then on, the jade became a national treasure. Later on, the Chu Kingdom proposed to the Zhao Kingdom and the jade was sent to the Zhao Kingdom as a gift.

In 283 BC, King Zhao of Qin（秦昭王）offered 15 cities to the

Zhao Kingdom in exchange for the jade（this is the origin of "价值连城"）. Lin Xiangru（蔺相如）, a minister in the Zhao Kingdom, understood that King Huiwen of Zhao（赵惠文王）did not wish to have such a priceless stone slip away from his hands, so he volunteered to go to the Qin court with the jade. On closer inspection, he thought the king of Qin did not want to keep his promise. Therefore he resolved not to give the jade to Qin. Stating that there was a tiny flaw in the jade, Lin Xiangru snatched it back and threatened to break both the jade and his bones if the Qin tried to take it back by force. The king of Qin, unwilling to see such a thing ruined by his actions, gave in for a moment. Lin Xiangru had the jade sent to the Zhao Kingdom at night secretly, thus giving birth to another Chinese idiom "完璧归赵", literally meaning "Returning the Jade Intact to Zhao", but extended to mean "returning something to its rightful owner".

In 221 BC, Qin conquered the other six states and founded the Qin Dynasty; He Shi Bi finally fell into the hands of Emperor Ying Zheng（秦王嬴政，Qin Shi Huang）, who ordered to have it made into his Imperial Seal（玉玺）. The words, "Having received the Mandate from Heaven, may (the emperor) lead a long and prosperous life"（受命于天，既寿永昌）were written by Li Si（李斯，Prime Minister of the Empire of Qin）. When Colonel Liu Bang（刘邦）attacked XianYang（咸阳）, Ziying（子婴）handed the jade over as a way of surrendering. This seal was passed on even as the dynasties rose and fell, but was lost in the Five Dynasties.

In English, the jade is called "turquoise". Do you know how it got its name? The word "turquoise" originates from a French word. It means Turkish stones for they were transported to Europe through Turkey. In fact, they came from Persia (Iran), a place where highly prized turquoise was produced. Stones range in color from sky blue to grayish green. High concentrations of iron create green turquoise, while the yellowish-green color is created by zinc and the blue color is created by copper.

In many cultures, this gemstone has been esteemed for thousands of years as a holy stone, a bringer of good fortune or a talisman. In the ancient Persian kingdom, the sky-blue gemstones were worn round the neck or wrist as protection against unnatural death. If they changed color, the wearer was thought to have reason to fear the approach of doom. In fact, the turquoise can certainly change color, but that is not necessarily a sign of impending danger. The change can be caused by the light, or by a chemical reaction brought about by cosmetics, dust or the acidity of the skin. Turquoise was even responsible for the material wellbeing of the wearer. A Persian scholar, for example, wrote: "The hand that wears a turquoise will never see poverty." In the West, Turquoise is the birthstone of December, symbolizing success and victory. I read that turquoise is the stone of the states, such as Arizona, Nevada and New Mexico. Is that true? Europeans believed that turquoise could preserve horses and riders from unexpected falls, and now they are regarded as the protective stone of tourists.

In modern gemstone therapy, people believe that wearing the stone would result in healing by the power of the earth's energies that were absorbed in the stone. Turquoise can also help detoxify the body, improve the thinking ability and strengthen a weak immune system. Those suffering from depression are recommended to wear a string of turquoise or a chain with turquoise beads. Its cheerful color is said to endow reticent personalities with more confidence. It is also often given as a gift, a stone of friendship, for the turquoise is said to be responsible for faithfulness and constancy in relationships.

Many tourists also buy them as an investment because they have elite status and become increasingly rare. But do you know how to protect them? As a general rule, we should protect them from the sunlight, heat and other chemicals, because they can dull the gemstone. Hairspray, perfumes and cosmetics can all affect the natural luster of turquoise.

VIII. Xuanyue Archway Scenic Zone

8.1 Xuanyue Archway

This is Xuanyue Archway, lying to the north of Wudang Mountain. In ancient times, it was the first gate to Wudang Mountain; people had to pass Xuanyue Archway, and Nanyan, if they started from Junzhou (which goes below the surface of the water because of the construction of Danjiangkou Reservoir) to Tianzhu Peak (the highest peak on Wudang Mountain). The total distance from Tianzhu Peak to Junzhou is 60 kilometers; the distance between Junzhou and Xuanyue Archway is 30 kilometers, the distance between Xuanyue Archway and Nanyan is 20 kilometers and the distance between Nanyan and Tianzhu Peak is 10 kilometers. 10, 20 and 30 coincide with Lao Tzu's theory that one produces two, two produces three and three produces everything.

The stone archway has four columns, three small archways and five roofs. It is 12 meters high and 12.4 meters wide. In Taoism, a place with five roofs and twelve-meter height refers to the immortals' residence. So when entering Xuanyue Archway, people had to be serious and behave themselves.

We can see four Chinese characters "Zhi Shi Xuan Yue" （治世玄

岳）, which were decreed by Emperor Jiajing in 1552. During Emperor Jiajing's reign, there existed political instability and social unrest. In this case, he wrote the four Chinese characters in the hope that he could rule the nation with Taoism ideology and with the help of Emperor Zhenwu.

This archway takes the shape of Paifang, which is a traditional Chinese architectural form. Originally Paifang served as a marker for the entrance of building complexes, such as mausoleums, temples, bridges, parks, or towns. Later, Paifang was built to function as decoration or commemorate virtuous people. Different designs in the beams of the Paifang are meant to carry various symbolic meanings. Look at the following examples:

(1) Dragon and Phoenix: Honored as the king of beasts, in ancient China the dragon symbolized the imperial power enjoyed by emperors, while the phoenix, honored as the queen of birds, was a token of the nobleness of queens in Chinese feudal society.

(2) Bat: The bat is a symbol of happiness because Fu, the Chinese word for bat, also sounds like the Chinese word for happiness. Therefore, bat designs could be frequently seen in ancient Paifang, which symbolized the five blessings of longevity, health, wealth, safety, and prosperity of offspring.

(3) Deer: The deer is a symbol of promotion and consequently wealth, because the Chinese translation for the word "deer" sounds like Lu, which in ancient China literally means the salary of an official and is a pun on the word for wealth.

(4) Fish: Along with a pond and lotus, the design of fish could

be commonly seen in Paifang, which is meant to convey the wish that people can enjoy a surplus, such as financial security, year after year. Also, in ancient China the design of "a carp swimming across waves" symbolized academic success in the imperial examination, as the carp is a good fortune symbol known for its legendary courage to swim against rapid currents.

In addition, carvings of some other animals like cranes, tortoises, and kylins (mythical composite creatures), and plants like pine, lotus, and peony, were also common themes to convey blessings of good fortune.

What's more, in ancient China with its rigid hierarchical system, it was necessary to build a Paifang through a set of complex procedures. The Paifang marking academic success in the imperial examination required the approval from local officials, while the Paifang marking one's chastity, benevolence, or virtue were not allowed to be built without the permission of emperors. Even the Paifang's size and style were determined according to one's social status.

8.2 Yuzhen Palace

Sitting at the foot of Wudang Mountain, Yuzhen Palace is one of the nine palaces at Wudang Mountain. It is 500 meters away from Xuanyue Archway and about 10 minutes' drive from the mountain gate.

It is said that Zhang Sanfeng, the founder of Tai Chi Quan, once refined himself here. Emperor Zhu Di ascended to the throne after raising a rebellion against his nephew. In order to win the hearts and minds of the people, he placed hope on Zhang Sanfeng, who, however, could be found nowhere. Although he failed in finding Zhang after many years of searching, Emperor Zhu Di ordered the construction of the palace to show his sincerity in 1412. Five years later, the palace was completed. It is the only palace built for a Taoist at Wudang Mountain. According to historical records, the Ming emperors never gave up searching for Zhang, but had no results.

During the reign of Emperor Jiajing, Yuzhen Palace had 396 rooms in its heyday. The 1935 flood, however, saw the palace turn into a courtyard. In 1996, a Kungfu academy was opened here at a rent of 15,000 yuan a year. Unfortunately, on January 19th, 2003, some important halls were burnt to ashes in a fire.

Because of the South-to-North Water Diversion Project（南水北调工程）, the Danjiangkou Dam will be heightened with the water level rising from 157 meters to 170 meters. With the height of 161 meters, the palace is facing the risk of being submerged. In order to protect the palace, three proposals were put forward: (1) raise the palace at the original site; (2) build a wall round the palace to retain the water; (3) move the palace to another place. A lot of investigations indicate that it is practical to raise the palace 15 meters and build a wall around the palace.

8.3 Yuxu Palace (Jade Void Palace)

This is Yuxu Palace. How did the palace get its name? It is said that when Emperor Zhenwu went up into Heaven, the Jade Emperor honored him with the title of Yuxu Master, so Emperor Yongle named it Yuxu Palace.

The palace was built in 1413 and restored in 1552. With a total number of 2,200 rooms (four pillars makes a room), it was the largest and most imposing building complex of that time. This place was a base camp during the construction period at Wudang Mountain, so people usually call it "Old Camp（老营）." In 1627, the palace got on a fire and the main buildings collapsed. 100 years later, it got on another fire and the attached buildings were ruined. The 1935 flood almost swallowed down all the relics.

Look! The layout is similar to that of the Palace Museum (Imperial Palace) in Beijing and it was an imperial palace in the south in the Ming Dynasty. Restricted by the topographical conditions, the palace faces northwest while other imperial palaces in China face south. Along both sides of the axis of the palace stood the Dragon-Tiger Hall, the Pilgrimage Hall, the Main Hall and the Parent Hall. In the courtyard stood four pavilions housing tablets on which the imperial edicts of Emperor Yongle were inscribed. The existing are two 1,036-meter-long walls, two pavilions, hall bases, the Parent Hall, etc. In 2001, it was listed as National Key Cultural Relics Protecting Unit.

The government attached great importance to the reconstruction of the palace. Since June 2007, 7 million yuan has been invested. It's said that in order to protect the ruins, Wuhan-Ankang Railway had to make a detour, which means an extra investment of 700 million had to be added and the project had to be put off for 9 months. In August 2009, the project of the main hall started, with a total investment of 12 million yuan.

IX. Wudang Museum

9.1 Introduction

Now we have arrived at the Wudang Museum. It was constructed in 2005 with a total investment of RMB 40 million yuan. It was officially opened in April 2008. The Wudang Museum covers an area of 6,200 square meters and has eight exhibition halls, displaying art of architecture, Taoist joss, Taoist history, wushu and regimen. It houses 2,000 pieces of cultural relics, among which 70 percent are under national first class protection.

This is the lobby. Look at the ceiling lamps, which seem to be in disorder. Do you know how they are arranged? Watch closely, and we can find that they are installed in accordance with the seven north mansions（北方七宿）of the 28 Lunar Mansions（二十八宿）—Dipper, Ox, Girl, Emptiness, Rooftop, Encampment and Wall（斗、牛、女、虚、危、室、壁）. The Twenty-eight Mansions are part of the Chinese constellations system. They can be considered as the equivalent to the zodiacal constellations（黄道十二宫）in the Western astronomy, though the Twenty-eight Mansions reflect the movement of the moon in a lunar month rather than the sun in a solar year. Ancient Chinese astronomers divided the sky ecliptic into four regions, collectively known as the Four Symbols（四象）, each assigned a mysterious animal. They are Azure Dragon（青龙）in the east, Black Tortoise（玄武）in the north, White Tiger（白虎）in the west, and Vermilion Bird（朱雀）in the south. Each region contains seven mansions, making a total of 28 mansions. The mansions are latitudes the Moon crosses during its monthly journey around Earth and serve as a way to track the Moon's progress.

In the 12th century (in the Song Dynasty), the tortoise-snake figure was personified as Xuanwu and received greater respect. In the 15th century, Zhu Di, a prince of the north, raised a rebellion, conquered the that-time capital—Nanjing and became an emperor. It's similar to Zhenwu, a prince of State Jingle, who was an emperor of the north, but refined himself and flew to Heaven on Wudang Mountain. Zhu Di declared that his imperial power was granted by Emperor Zhenwu. Therefore, Zhenwu enjoyed the highest status on Wudang Mountain.

On this platform stand the statues of Six Jia（六甲星神）. They serve as guardians, protecting Emperor Zhenwu. They belong to the six stars of Ziweiyuan（紫微垣, the Purple Forbidden Enclosure）.

9.2 Architecture Hall

In 1994, the ancient building complex at Wudang Mountain was included into the World Cultural Heritage List by UNESCO. These are the comments made by the experts of UNESCO after their inspections in 1994: (1) "Mt. Wudang area is certainly one of the most beautiful areas in the world because it combines ancient wisdom, historic architecture and natural beauty."—Kaosia, expert of UNESCO; (2) "The great past of China is still solid in Mountain Wudang."—Sumimtardia, expert of UNESCO; (3) "The paradise in the world and occupied a more prominent position than the other five national famed mountains."—Yang Tingbao, Vice-chairman of the World Architect Association.

Here we can see some glazed tiles. They don't absorb water, so they are used to prevent water from entering the halls and ensure the stability of the roof.

This model was made in Beijing in 1616. It miniaturizes the landscape of Wudang Mountain. On its top is the Golden Hall. We can see five figures with dragon's face and human's body, representing the five dragons which supported Zhenwu to Heaven.

Here we can see Yujichi Pavilion （禹迹亭，Pavilion for Great Yu）. It was built to commemorate Great Yu（大禹）. Great Yu was a legendary ruler in ancient China. He was famous for his introduction of flood control and for his upright moral character. Almost all the Chinese know the story about him. It's said that the Chinese heartland was frequently plagued by floods that prevented further economic and social development during the reign of King Yao（尧帝）. Yu's father, Gun（鲧）, was tasked with devising a system to control the flooding. He spent more than nine years building a series of dikes and dams along the riverbanks, but all of this was ineffective, despite the great number and size of these dikes. As an adult, Yu continued his father's work and made a careful study of the river systems in an attempt to learn why his father's great efforts had failed. Instead of directly damming the rivers' flow, Yu made a system of irrigation canals which relieved floodwater into fields, as well as spending great effort dredging the riverbeds. Yu is said to have eaten and slept with the common workers and spent most of his time personally assisting the work of dredging the silty beds of the rivers for the 13 years the projects took to complete. The dredging and irrigation were successful, and allowed ancient Chinese culture to flourish along the Yellow River, Wei River, and other waterways of the Chinese heartland. The project earned Yu renown throughout Chinese history, and is referred to in Chinese history as "Great Yu Controls the Waters"（大禹治水）.

This sandstone base, formerly in Nanyan Palace, was used for supporting an incense burner. It is the only preserved sandstone carving.

This part is called Chiwen（螭吻）. "Chi" means hornless dragon or young dragon and "Wen" means animals' mouth, so it literally means hornless-dragon mouth. It is one of the Nine Young Dragons in imperial roof decorations and an ornamental motif in traditional Chinese architecture and art. It's said that dragon gives birth to nine young dragons, which are traditional Chinese architectural decorations. The Chiwens are placed on both ends of the ridgepoles of roofs to swallow all evil influences. In Fengshui theory, a Chiwen or Chiwei supposedly protects against not only fire, but also flood and typhoon. Structurally, Chiwen is located at the junction of roof ridges, so it can prevent water from entering the halls. Since the 15th century, a sword has been pricked into it tightly for fear that it would run away. Some say that the sword can frighten the ghosts away. In fact, the sword is used for decorating the roof and connecting the parts.

Here we can see a copy of a stone Paifang built in 1553. The characters "Zhi Shi Xuan Yue" mean that Emperor Jiajing hoped to rule the nation with Taoism ideology and with the help of Emperor Zhenwu. In 1988, it was classified as one of the third group of national key cultural sites under the state protection by the State Council. The characters were carved on both sides of the gate, which mean that all people are equal.

In terms of raw material, Paifang can be made of stone, brick, or fine wood. Function-wise, many a Paifang was erected to serve as directions, decorate the neighboring community, and honor and commemorate venerable people or historic events. In the past, "Chastity Paifangs"（贞节坊）were given to the widows who remained unmarried till death, praising what was seen as loyalty to their deceased husbands.

Outside of China, Paifang has long been the symbol of Chinatowns. The largest Paifang outside of China can be found at Washington D.C.'s Chinatown.

Now we can see 300,000 laborers were working hard to build temples and palaces at Wudang Mountain in 1412. They spent 12 years working here. On both sides are their living quarters and in the middle they were working on Bixi（赑屃）, which carried imperial edicts.

Among the articles granted by emperors, an inscribed board cut with an imperial decree in 1413 is the most precious. The imperial decree is the earliest one about Wudang Mountain kept until now. It reads "Many Taoists refine themselves on Mt. Taihe（太和山，武当山）and they need absolute quietness; those who harass the Taoists should be punished severely. If a Taoist makes trouble instead of devoting himself to refinement, minor offenders should be expelled from Mt. Taihe, while heavy ones should be reported to me and receive tough punishment. October 18th, Yongle 11th." It was a law made by Emperor Yongle. It is also an essential document proving. Wudang Mountain received considerable attention from emperors. According to Zhu Jiatao（朱家溍）, an expert from the Palace Museum, 83 procedures were used to produce it. Its frame is decorated with nine dragons.

Do you know what it is called? It is Dougong（斗拱）. Dougong is a part of the wooden structure of traditional Chinese building because the walls in these structures are not load-bearing. Walls function to divide spaces rather than support weight. The function of Dougong is to transfer the weight on crossbeams to the vertical columns. The more sets of Dougong, the more weight it can transfer. It also allows structures to be elastic and withstand damage from earthquakes. In the 15th century, a new wooden component replaced Dougong and Dougong became smaller and more numerous, which made the building more graceful instead of supporting the roof.

Here are four stone-carved monks' statues. They originally stood in the four directions of Bu'er's Pagoda（不二塔）behind Zhanqi Peak. Bu'er was a Buddhist monk's name. Bu'er means being persistent. He came to Wudang Mountain to refine himself without giving up.

After his death, he was buried in the holy land of Taoism, so it is a good example to show the combination between Buddhism and Taoism.

Can you see a rising and a falling dragon here? Do you know its name and functions? It's called Zhaobi(照壁), also known as a "spirit wall". In ancient China, a solitary wall usually facing the front gate was built inside or outside the courtyard to block the view of the rest of the courtyard and prevent ghosts from entering the house. In terms of material, it can be made of glaze, brick, stone, wood, etc. This is made of stone.

Queti（雀替）is a Chinese term in architecture. It is installed in the intersection between the horizontal girder and vertical column. It functions to support the weight and decorate the building. It can also show the high status of the owner. The left one is a pair of wood carved kylins and the right is a pair of wood carved lions. Besides the two, there are a plenty of forms, such as dragon, phoenix, crane, deer, lion, and kylin. They are the original ones.

9.3 Celebrity Hall

There are many famous persons at Wudang Mountain.

9.3.1 Lao Tzu: Lao Tzu lived in the 6th century BC, and was a great philosopher, thinker, educator and the founder of the Taoist school of thought in ancient China. Lao Tzu is an honorific title（尊称）. Lao means "venerable" or "old", such as modern Mandarin Laoshi or teacher. Zi was used in ancient China as an honorific suffix, indicating "Master", or "Sir". According to historical documents, Lao

Tzu was a learned, sharp-eyed, forethoughtful, and eloquent wise man, which might have something to do with his experience as a historiographer in charge of the libraries of the Eastern Zhou Dynasty (770BC-256BC).

The biggest achievement of Lao Tzu is his book *Tao Te Ching* (Classic of the Way and Its Power), and it is said that *Tao Te Ching*, the most frequently translated work in world literature next to the *Bible* (《圣经》), is also regarded as one of the three works which greatly influence the thoughts of the Chinese, together with the *Book of Changes* (《易经》) and *The Analects of Confucius* (《论语》).

Study *Tao Te Ching* and the *Bible*, and people are often struck by the similarities between them. For example, (1) The *Bible* says, "Those who live by the sword will die by the sword." Chapter 74 of *Tao Te Ching* says, "People who try to take the executioner's place are like people that try to take the Master Carpenter's place. If you use the Master's tools, you just cut your own hands." (2) The *Bible* says, "Blessed are the meek, for they shall inherit the earth." Chapter 76 of *Tao Te Ching* says, "The soft and yielding (people) will prevail." (3) The *Bible* says, "The more you talk, the more you are likely to sin. If you are wise, you will keep quiet." Chapter 5 of *Tao Te Ching* says, "The mouth, on the other hand, becomes exhausted if you talk too much. Better to keep your thoughts inside you." As the Buddha says, "Truth is true in all places and times and applies to all people." It isn't surprising then, that wise people in different times and places made the same observations about life. (Adapted from http://www.thetao.info/tao/christ.htm)

Tao Te Ching is actually a 5,000-word philosophical poem in verses, which consists of two parts: *Daojing*（《道经》）emphasizes on the harmony between the individual and the cosmos while *Dejing* （《德经》）emphasizes on how to achieve the harmony. *Daojing* is the aim and *Dejing* is the methods. *Daojing* is hardware and *Dejing* is software.

Early in the Western Han Dynasty (206BC-8AD), the ruling class practiced a kind of so-called Huanglao (Emperor Huang and Lao Tzu) politics, characterized by Taoist doctrine of governing by doing nothing, and realized a quick economic instauration, known as reigns of Wen & Jing（文景之治，prosperity in the period of Emperor Wen and Emperor Jing）in history.

9.3.2 Zhuangzi: Zhuangzi, with the given name of Zhou, lived between 369BC-286BC. He was another representative of Taoist school of thought after Lao Tzu, as well as an excellent litterateur and philosopher. He expatiated on the essence of Taoist thought and developed the Taoist theory in his book *Zhuangzi*, and made it a philosophical school with a profound influence on later generations.

Zhuangzi was born in a poor family, lived primarily on making straw sandals, and was once an official in charge of painting work. However, he was quite learned through studying the thought of all kinds of schools. In his lifetime, Zhuangzi was indifferent to fame and gain, which seemed to him like devils rather than angels, and had long pursued spiritual freedom. At that time, the King of the Chu State heard about his incredible scholarship, and tried to invite him to be a high-ranked official. Unexpectedly, Zhuangzi refused completely by saying, "Get out of here and don't humiliate me! I would rather live happily like a tortoise in the pond than be limited by the king! I won't be an official in my lifetime, and I will be free for ever!"

The book *Zhuangzi*, as an important part of Taoist works, consists of 33 articles, including *Neipian* (《内篇》, inner section), *Waipian*(《外篇》, outer section)and *Zapian*(《杂篇》, mixed section). It is generally believed that *Neipian* was written by Zhuangzi himself, but the other two were done by his pupils and his other followers. It uses numerous parables to explain the complicated philosophy, and is of high literary value due to its aesthetic beauty in words.

9.3.3 Yinxi: Yinxi, a high-ranked official in the Zhou Dynasty, was good at astrology. Once when he was observing the astronomical phenomenon, he found purple clouds floating from the east and predicted that a wise man would go through Hanguguan Pass (函谷关). Later, Lao Tzu approached Hanguguan Pass on an ox. He went to greet him with his subordinates and asked Lao Tzu to teach him the Tao. Then Lao Tzu stayed there and wrote a 5,000-word book, *Tao Te Ching.*

After he got the book, he pretended to be ill and stopped working for the government. He went to Wudang Mountain and refined himself in a cliff, Yixi Cliff (尹喜岩). When Lao Tzu heard this, he came to Wudang Mountain on an ox to visit Yinxi, and the two started their traveling without further information.

9.3.4 Emperor Taizong: As early as the Tang Dynasty (618-907), Wudang Mountain attracted emperors' attention. During the reign of Emperor Taizong, there was a drought; he sent someone to pray for rain on Wudang Mountain, and it succeeded. In order to commemorate it, the first site of worship—the Five Dragon Temple—was constructed.

9.3.5 Zhu Di: The Yongle Emperor was born Zhu Di in 1360, the fourth son of Zhu Yuanzhang, the first emperor of the Ming Dynasty. Zhu Di was entitled as the Prince of Yan（燕王）, the area around Beijing. When Zhu Di moved to Beijing, he found a city that had been devastated by famine and disease and that was under threat of invasion from Mongols from the north.

Zhu Di had been very successful against the Mongols and impressed his father with his energy, risk-taking ability and leadership. But Zhu Di was not the oldest brother, forcing his father to name Zhu Biao（朱标）as crown prince. When Zhu Biao died of illness in 1392, his son Zhu Yunwen（朱允炆）, the son of the late Zhu Biao, was crowned as the Jianwen Emperor. Zhu Di and Jianwen began a deadly feud. When Zhu Di traveled with his guards to pay tribute to his father, Jianwen took his actions as a threat and sent troops to repel him. Zhu Di was forced to leave in humiliation. He found himself in a political gridlock; his rebellion slowly began to take shape. In 1399, Zhu Di raised a rebellion, known as the Jingnan Campaign（靖难之役）. He was a great military commander and led his army enter the capital city, Nanjing. In the widespread panic caused by the sudden entry, the emperor's palace caught fire. Zhu Yunwen and his wife disappeared, most likely falling victim to the fire.

Zhu Di is considered an architect and keeper of Chinese culture, history, and statecraft and an influential ruler in Chinese history. He moved the capital from Nanjing to Beijing where it was located in the following generations, and constructed the Forbidden City there. After its dilapidation and disuse during the Yuan Dynasty and Hongwu's reign, the Yongle Emperor had the Grand Canal（大运河）of China repaired and reopened in order to supply the new capital of Beijing in the north with a steady flow of goods and southern food supplies. He commissioned most of the exploratory sea voyages of Zheng He（郑和）. During his reign the monumental *Yongle Encyclopedia*（《永乐大典》）was completed. Although his father Zhu Yuanzhang was reluctant to do so when he was emperor, Yongle upheld the civil service examinations for drafting educated government officials instead of using simple recommendation and appointment.

He is remembered very much for his cruelty, just like his father. He killed most of the Jianwen palace servants, tortured many Jianwen Emperor loyalists to death, killed or by other means badly treated their relatives. In 1420, he ordered 2,800 ladies-in-waiting to a slow slicing death（凌迟）, and watched, because he thought one of his favourite concubine had been poisoned. Zhu Di is known for ordering perhaps the only case of "extermination of the ten agnates"（诛十族）in the history of China. For nearly 1,500 years of feudal China, the nine exterminations（诛九族）is considered one of the most severe punishments found in traditional Chinese law. Just before the accession of Emperor Yongle, prominent historian Fang Xiaoru（方孝孺）refused to write the inaugural address and therefore aggravated the Emperor. He was recorded as saying in defiance to the would-be

Emperor: "莫说九族，十族何妨！" ("Never mind nine agnates, go ahead with ten!"). Thus he was granted his wish with perhaps the only and infamous case of "extermination of ten agnates" in the history of China. In addition to the blood relations from his nine-agnate family hierarchy, his students and peers were added to be the 10th group.

9.3.6 Emperor Kangxi: Kangxi was the longest-reigning Chinese emperor in history. He is also considered as one of China's greatest emperors.

In 1690, Emperor Kangxi ordered to repair Taizipo Palace, which was damaged during the battle against Wu Sangui. Two five-meter-high steles were built and used for recording the events.

In 1703, Emperor Kangxi wrote five plaques and had them sent to Wudang Mountain. Jin Guang Miao Xiang, the only existing one, is now inside the Golden Hall. The others, however, can be found nowhere.

9.3.7 Chen Tuan: Chen Tuan lived to be 118 years. He was a quick learner, but failed the imperial examination many times. He lost hope in becoming a government official and began to visit places of interest. Influenced by many Taoists, he refined himself on Wudang Mountain and Huashan Mountain, studying *Book of Changes*. He advocated preserving health by sleeping; he could sleep for several days without eating or drinking. He was also a calligrapher; there were two Chinese characters "福" (Fortune) and "寿" (Longevity) written by him on the wall of Nanyan Palace.

According to historical records, he was popular with the

commons; he also became the favorite of emperors of different dynasties. In 984, Emperor Taizong of the Song Dynasty invited him to the court, asking him how to live long. Chen Tuan always beat around the bush, which made him more mysterious. Emperor Taizong entitled him Mr. Xiyi（希夷先生）. Xi means shutting one's eyes to something and Yi means turning a deaf ear to something. Mr. Xiyi means Chen Tuan was indifferent to worldly affairs.

Chen Tuan died in a cave on Huashan Mountain. It is said that his body kept warm even seven days after his death.

9.3.8 Xu Xiake: In 1623, Xu Xiake toured Wudang Mountain and recorded what he had seen, heard and investigated at Wudang Mountain.

Xu Xiake (1587-1641) was a noted traveler and geographer of the late Ming Dynasty (1368-1644). He was born in Jiangsu Province. He studied the ancient classics as a small boy, but failed the imperial examination at the age of 15. Then he buried himself in historical books and the books on different places, and devoted himself to traveling all over the country. At the age of 19, his father died. He planned to stay at home, accompanying his mother, but his mother was so understanding that she encouraged him to realize his dream.

From then on, Xu Xiake traveled around and conducted surveys in 16 provinces. In conducting his surveys, he would never blindly embrace the conclusions recorded in previous documents; he corrected some mistakes of the records on the source and waterways of Chinese rivers. For example, the documentations made by his predecessors in their geographical studies believed that the source of the Changjiang River was the Minjiang River（岷江）. After investigations, he discovered that it should be the Jinshajiang River （金沙江）.

Xu was a pioneer in systematic karst studies in both China and the world. He visited over 270 caves in Guangxi, Guizhou and Yunnan provinces, kept records of their directions, height, and depth, and elaborated on the cause of the formation. It was more than 100 years after his death that Europeans began to survey the landform.

Xu Xiake's contribution to the ancient Chinese geography was unprecedented; he wrote a 20-million-word diary. Unfortunately, only 0.4 million words still remain. His travel journal was compiled by the later generations into a book called *Travel Diaries of Xu Xiake*（《徐霞客游记》）, which is of high scientific and literary value.

9.3.9 Zhu Bai: Zhu Bai was one of Emperor Zhu Yuanzhang's sons. Zhu Yuanzhang was the first emperor of the Ming Dynasty. During the reign of Zhu Yunwen, the third emperor of the Ming Dynasty, he began to suppress feudal lords. Zhu Bai, his uncle, felt threatened, came to Wudang Mountain with ritual instruments used in Taoist mass—a golden dragon, a jade circle and stone inscriptions （金龙、玉壁和山简）during the Lantern Festival in 1399. It was believed that these instruments could be used to send his wishes to Emperor Zhenwu. Zhu Bai buried these instruments on Wudang Mountain in the hope that they could help him escape from disasters. Unfortunately, several months later, under Emperor Zhu Yunwen's pressure, he burned himself in a fire. In 1982, the three instruments were found in Zixiao Palace. Zhu Yunwen's reign was short

(1398-1402); these instruments were precious.

9.4 Wudang Taoist Josses

There are thousands of Taoist josses under the national first class culture relics. In the middle are Zhenwu's 13 statues of different shapes, postures, ages, sizes and materials. Interestingly, all the statues share the common feature that Emperor Zhenwu has a full-moon-like face, bare feet and unrolled hair.

This is a jade-made statue of Emperor Zhenwu. With hands on Dantian（丹田）, a center of Qi or life force energy, he is refining himself. Usually, a person closes his eyes during self-cultivation practice in order to concentrate his mind. But why does he open his eyes? According to Qigong experts, this method is called "Light-eating Method "（吃光法）. He opens his eyes to absorb the essence of sun and moon.

Here we can see nine gilded bronze statues. They are deities of nine stars. From the left to the right, they are Ri Yao（日曜）, Yue Yao （月曜）, Huo Yao（火曜）, Shui Yao（水曜）, Mu Yao（木曜）, Jin Yao（金曜）, Tu Yao（土曜）, Ji Yao（计曜）and Luo Hou（罗睺）. In ancient China, some regarded them as the nine stars in the Big Dipper. Do you know how many stars the Big Dipper is made up of? There are seven visible stars and two invisible "attendant" stars. Legend has it that there used to be 9 stars（北斗九星）but 2 faded and that those who were lucky enough to see the 2 dim stars would prolong his life. Some held different views. Legend has it that an empress was pregnant and hoped that she would have children capable enough to help her husband rule the nation. One day in spring, she gave birth to nine buds, which turned into nine sons. Two of them became emperors and the others became the seven stars in the Big Dipper. She is regarded as Goddess Doumu in Taoism.

This is the statue of Guan Yu. Are you familiar with *Romance of the Three Kingdoms* (《三国演义》)? Guan Yu, the sworn brother of Liu Bei and Zhang Fei, was famous for being loyal, righteous, faithful, wise, benevolent and courageous. Guan Yu was deified as early as the Sui Dynasty (581-618), and is still popularly worshiped today among the Chinese people. He is worshiped as an indigenous Chinese deity, a bodhisattva in Buddhist tradition and as a guardian deity in Taoism. He is also held in high esteem in Confucianism. Today, many shrines to Guan Yu are found in homes or businesses. In Hong Kong, a shrine for Guan is located in each police station. Interestingly, criminals also pay respect to Guan Yu. Guan Yu is also worshiped by Chinese businessmen in Shanxi, Hong Kong, and Macau as a wealth god, since he is perceived to bless the upright and protect them from the wicked. Guan Yu is traditionally portrayed as a red-faced warrior with a long lush beard. The idea of his red face could have been borrowed from opera representation, where red faces depict loyalty and righteousness. In the Western world, Guan Yu is sometimes called the Taoist God of War, probably because he is one of the most well-known military generals worshiped by the Chinese people. This is a misconception of his role, as, unlike Mars, Guan Yu, as a god, does not necessarily bless those who go to battle but rather people who observe the code of brotherhood and righteousness.

This is a wood-carved statue of Lao Tzu. In the middle are the statues of Lao Tzu and his twelve disciples. They were used to be gilded, but the gold leaf virtually falls off as many years have gone by.

The statue of Zhenwu was donated by the local believers in the Ming Dynasty. Usually, the statue with a back niche is often seen in Buddhism, but seldom seen in Taoism. This statue can show us the combination of Buddhism and Taoism.

9.5 Brief History of Taoism (I)

9.5.1 Lao Tzu riding on a black ox: This is Lao Tzu. He was from State Chu in the Spring and Autumn Period during the 6th century BC. In Taoism, he is considered an incarnation of the "Senior Lord of the Supreme"（太上老君）. It is said that the Pass Commissioner Yinxi felt the presence of a purple mist suddenly appearing in the sky and surmised that a great sage was passing through the area. Not long thereafter appeared Lao Tzu riding on his black ox from the east. Yinxi implored Lao Tzu to write down a book for later generations. Lao Tzu consented and wrote the famous *Tao Te Ching* in 5,000 characters. After finishing it, he got on his ox and rode off to the west with no further information.

9.5.2 Hu Bi Picture: This is called Hu Bi Picture（扈跸图）. Hu means attendants, and Bi means imperial coach. In the middle is Emperor Zhenwu and on both sides are the attendants.

9.5.3 Vase: Look at the vase. Its mouth is decorated with lotus. Do you know the name of the animal with a ring in its mouth? It's called Chi（螭）. Chi is one of Dragon's sons, who likes swallowing. The body of the vase is decorated with an animal, which loves to eat and is found on food-related wares. It's called Taotie（饕餮）, also one of Dragon's sons.

9.5.4 Longevity shrine（寿龛）: Do you know what it is used for? It's used as a coffin by a Taoist monk. This method is called Zuo Gang（坐缸, sitting in the jar）. It is still used by some pious Buddhists and Taoists. In 2000, in Shangrao County（上饶县）, Jiangxi Province, a villager dealt with his father's body in this way, according to his father's will. After seating the body, they filled the jar with charcoal and lime powder in yellow paper, and then covered it with another jar. At last, the jar was sealed with a liquid mixture of Chinese wood oil and lime powder. In this way, the body does not tend to become decayed. Three years later, he took out his father's body and painted it with salt lime, and then a real-body statue came into being. It is a waste of land, and against the moral ethics. Besides, it costs more than cremation. Therefore, the practice is not encouraged.

9.5.5 Seven-star lotus lamp（七星莲花灯）: The lamp is used as a ritual instrument when offering sacrifices to Heaven. What do you call the flower? Lotus. In Taoism, lotus is one of Hidden Eight Immortals（暗八仙）, held by He Xiangu. In Buddhism, it is one of the Eight Auspicious Symbols. Buddha is sometimes depicted sitting on a lotus flower, symbolizing the one who overcomes the pain that prevails in the material world and becomes enlightened, just like the lotus flower, which starts to grow in the dirty and muddy water but manages to surpass the water and produce a perfect flower. The water, in many different belief systems, represents the material world, or the physical realm. A Chinese scholar Zhou Dunyi（周敦颐）said, "I love the lotus because while growing from mud, it is unstained." In China, lotus has rich connotations: 1) As early as in the *Classic of Poetry* (《诗经》), which was written 3,000 years ago, there have been writings associating lotus with beauty. 2) It is also used to describe the constancy of love between couples. Though the lotus root breaks, the two parts may still link with each other through fibers of lotus root. 3) In Chinese, the word for lotus is pronounced "HE," the same as the word which means harmony. So in folk paintings, the images of two fairies, holding a lotus and a box in their hands, are used to symbolize auspiciousness and harmony. 4) In Chinese, the word for a lotus of a light blue color（青莲）is pronounced similarly to the word for rectitude. The lotus is used to illustrate an official's incorruptibility.

9.5.6 Incense Burner: Here we can see two vases, two candle sticks and an incense burner, which were all used for offering sacrifices to Heaven. Incense burner evolved from Ding（鼎）, which used to be made in two shapes with round vessels with three legs and rectangular ones with four legs. In ancient times, Ding was originally a kind of cooking vessel. Perhaps the most famous ancient Dings were said to have been cast by Great Yu（大禹）of the Xia Dynasty. They were used to symbolize the Jiuzhou（九洲）or Nine Provinces which Great Yu divided his territory into. In the Shang and Zhou Dynasties, Ding had changed from the cooking vessel to the ritual vessel. Gradually, it became the symbol of supreme power and dignity. Officials with different ranks were allowed to have different numbers of Dings; only emperors were entitled to have nine Dings. The whereabouts of the nine Dings are presently unknown, but are said to have been lost during the imperial Qin Dynasty (221BC-206 BC).

9.5.7 Hua Gu（花瓠）: The vase, called Hua Gu, was one of the five ritual vessels. The five vessels include two vases, two Hua Gus and an incense burner. It originated from the Yuan Dynasty (13th century), and was popular from the 14th to 18th centuries. During its early period, it was used for decoration; the commons put some flowers in it.

9.5.8 Candle stick（蜡台）: This gold inlaid candle stick is also used when offering sacrifices to Heaven. The middle part is decorated with the Hidden Eight Immortals (the talismans held by the Eight Immortals) and the symbol of 卍 (representing lucky happiness).

9.5.9 Holy Tablet of Emperor Xuantian（武当山玄天上帝圣牌）: This was bestowed to Nanyan Palace on Wudang Mountain in 1524 by Emperor Jiajing. It has five colors, and the main colors are yellow, green and blue. In the lower part, we can see two phoenixes and the sun. In the center are nine Chinese characters "Wu Dang Shan Xuan Tian Shang Di Sheng Pai"（武当山玄天上帝圣牌）. How many dragons can you see? There are five dragons. They are the dragons which supported Zhenwu to Heaven in Nanyan. It was made in Town of Jingde, known as the "Porcelain Capital" because it has been producing quality pottery for 1,700 years. Different carving techniques were used. Now it is under the national protection. The unique shape of the holy tablet makes it different from ancestral tablets of either the royalties or the folks. By now it has been the second-to-none Taoist spirit tablet with very high historic value.

9.6 Brief History of Taoism (II)

The history of Taoism stretches throughout Chinese history. The acceptance of Taoism by the ruling class has waxed and waned, alternately enjoying periods of favor and rejection.

Taoism's origins may be traced to a religious group named Five Dou Rice (五斗米道, later called Zhengyi school) founded by Zhang Daoling (2nd century AD), who claimed that Lao Tzu enlightened him in the year 142. It is said that the one who wanted to be a member of the group needed to hand in five dous of rice (one dou equals to 10 liters).

Taoism gained official status in China during the Tang Dynasty, whose emperors respected Lao Tzu as their ancestor, claiming that they had the same surname as Lao Tzu, Li Er. Emperor Xuanzong (685-762), who ruled at the height of the Tang Dynasty, wrote commentaries on *Tao Te Ching*. The Gaozong Emperor added *Tao Te Ching* to the list of classics (经) to be studied for the imperial examinations.

In the Song Dynasty, Taoism came to a prosperous stage. On the one hand, the Song government made use of Taoism to consolidate its power. On the other hand, the government also limited the number of Taoist temples and palaces to ensure the number of working force. The Quanzhen School of Taoism was founded during this period. The

Quanzhen School and the Zhengyi School are the two schools of Taoism that have survived to the present. Confucianism, Taoism, and Buddhism were consciously synthesized.

In the Yuan Dynasty, Taoism suffered a significant setback in 1281 when all copies of *Daozang*（《道藏》）were ordered burned. But things took a turn for better when Qiu Chuji （丘处机）, a famous Taoist monk, was invited by Genghis Khan（成吉思汗）to share the secret medicine of immortality. He explained the Taoist philosophy and the ways to prolong life and was honest in saying there was no secret medicine of immortality. Genghis Khan honored him with the title of "Spirit Immortal"（邱神仙）and also made Qiu Chuji in charge of all religious persons in the empire.

In the Ming Dynasty, Taoism reached its peak. In 1406, Ming emperor Zhu Di commanded that all Taoist texts be collected and combined into a new version of *Daozang*. The text was finally finished in 1447, and took nearly forty years to complete.

In the Qing Dynasty, the Qing government returned the Confucian classics to favor and completely rejected Taoism.

9.7 Pilgrimage Culture

9.7.1 Sword: Do you know what the sword is used for? It is used to lock your mouth. Are you surprised? When parents have been ill for a long time, the believer will take a bath, wear new clothes and pierce his cheek with a sword. On the way to Wudang Mountain, he does not eat or drink anything. When he reaches the Golden Hall of Wudang Mountain, he burns incense and worships Emperor Zhenwu.

Then the sword can be taken off and some incense ashes can be applied to the injuries in order to stop bleeding. The custom still exists.

9.7.2 Dragon-Head Incense: In Nanyan Palace, there is a stone sculpture called Dragon-Head Incense Burner. It is 3 meters long and 0.55 meters wide. On the head of the dragon, there is an incense burner; under it is a deep valley. In ancient times, many people risked their lives to burn incense here to show their piety. It was so dangerous that thousands of people died, so during the reign of Emperor Kangxi in the Qing Dynasty, people were forbidden to burn incense here.

9.7.3 500 guardian deities: We can see some wood-carved guardian deities (Lingguan officials). Their clothes can tell us whether they are military or civil officials. On Wudang Mountain, statues of guardian deities made of different materials, such as iron, copper, stone and wood, can all be found. The head of the guardian deities is Wang Shan（王善）. In Taoism, he usually stands at the mountain gate.

9.7.4. Umbrella for pilgrimage purpose（万民伞）: What can you see here? We can see an umbrella. Do you know what are on the pieces of the cloth? They are the believers' names. In this way, the believers think that they can pray to Emperor Zhenwu to bless them. Under the umbrella, there is an incense burner. The believers will keep the incense burning and music playing on the way to the Golden Hall. The pilgrims are forbidden to say anything evil or anything that may offend the deities. The pilgrims usually flock to Wudang

Mountain on March 3rd of the lunar calendar (Zhenwu's birthday) and September 9th of the lunar calendar (the day when Zhenwu flew to Heaven). They also worship Emperor Zhenwu on January 1st of the lunar calendar in the hope that they will be lucky and happy in the coming new year.

9.8 Wushu and Regimen

Have you ever seen the film *Karate Kid* (*Kungfu Dream*)? It is a 2010 American martial arts drama film and remake of the 1984 film of the same name. The film was directed by Harald Zwart, starring Jaden Smith and Jackie Chan. Part of the film was shot at Wudang Mountain. The plot concerns a 12-year-old boy from Detroit who moved to Beijing with his mother and got to know a girl. The friendship between him and the girl brought him some troubles; he was bullied by his neighborhood. Luckily, he was saved by an aging maintenance man, Mr. Han, a Kungfu master, who later taught him the secrets to self-defense. Finally, he won the championship in a Wushu competition.

There are several terms which may seem confusing: Kungfu, Wushu and Qigong. Kungfu is often used in the West to refer to Chinese martial arts, also known as Wushu. Wushu literally means "martial art". It contains two aspects: 1) strength and skills; 2) moral virtues. A Wushu master always puts more emphasis on moral virtues than strength and skills, which is the essence of Chinese Wushu. Wushu embodies a profound philosophy and a sense of human life and social values. The origin of Wushu may be traced back to prehistoric times when our ancestors used stones and wooden clubs in hunting, both for subsistence and self-defence. In tribal strife, they used their tools of production as weapons of war. During the Shang (17th-11th centuries BC) and Zhou (11th century BC-221BC) Dynasties, with the development of productive forces, especially that of the techniques in bronze casting, the weapon varieties increased and their quality improved. At the end of the Eastern Han Dynasty (in the second century), Hua Tuo developed the game by imitating the gestures of tigers, deer, bears, apes and cranes for the purpose of improving strength, activating the joints and the blood flow. In the Jin and Southern and Northern Dynasties, Wushu came under the influence of Buddhism and Taoism. In the Tang Dynasty, Empress Wu Zetian set up a court examination system to choose military talents and advocated both military men and scholars to practice Wushu.

Qigong began as a form of ancient dance believed to remove stagnation and obstruction in the body. In ancient China, people believed there were two kinds of Qi; one is pre-celestial, the other is post-celestial. The pre-celestial energy is the root of all creation. The purpose of Qigong is to transform the post-celestial generative energy (Qi) back into its pre-celestial state (Qi) through proper breathing and diet so that one can preserve health and prolong his or her lifespan. Qigong can be categorized into two: Dynamic and static. Dynamic Qigong can be easily recognized as a series of carefully choreographed movements or gestures that are designed to promote and manipulate the flow of Qi within the practitioner's body. Tai Chi Quan, a Chinese martial art, is a well-known representation of dynamic Qigong. Other examples include Five Animal Frolics, White Crane Qigong, and Wild Goose Qigong（五禽戏、白鹤功和大雁功）where the practitioner mimics motions of animals. Static Qigong is performed by holding a certain posture, position or stance for a period of time, breathing in and out, imagining that Qi flows smoothly and continuously through the practitioner. It came from the same roots as Tai Chi Quan. Tai Chi Quan is a "soft" or "internal" martial art that relies on inner strength and the movement of Qi guided by the mind. The movements can be adapted for fighting. Qigong is not a martial art, but a healing art. It is thought that Qigong was used to help warriors build and focus energy and increase strength, stamina and coordination.

More than 300 different known martial arts styles are practiced in China. There are two Chinese martial art systems, the internal system from Wudang Mountain and the external system from Henan Province. Wudang Mountain is the birthplace of the internal Taoist martial arts. There is a Chinese saying "In North China people advocate Shaolin Kungfu, while in South China people respect Wudang Kungfu."

Ever since its beginning, Wudang Kungfu has had a close relationship with Taoism; a Taoist practitioner cultivates his mind by practicing Wudang Kungfu. What a Taoist practitioner pursues is to keep healthy and prolong his lifespan. This is the reason why Taoism has formed a wealth of exercises, knowledge and even sciences on regimen and health preservation.

A Taoist practitioner may achieve his goal by different ways, such as massaging, bathing in fragrant water, absorbing and digesting Qi instead of grains, making immortality elixirs inside his body, taking Chinese herbs, practicing Qigong and Wudang Kungfu. Now a Taoist practitioner attaches great importance to the use of Qi, which is Qigong. Qigong exercises help develop "the Three Regulations": Xing（形, posture）, Yi（意, consciousness）, and Qi（气, vital energy or breath）. The Chinese believe that a balance between these three elements brings physical, mental, and spiritual well-being.

Qigong may focus on consciousness, posture and breath. One skill of Qigong is to practice breathing exercises. Stand, sit or lie down. Relax the body，relieve the mind, get rid of stray thoughts and concentrate on the Dantian. Breathe in through the nose as if filling your belly with Qi and out through the mouth, with your mouth slightly open. Collapse your belly as you exhale slowly. The breaths should be slow, but natural. Continue until you achieve a natural rhythm. Eventually, you will breathe fewer times per minute. This is called "tortoise breathing"（龟吸法）.

The name "Tai Chi Quan" is held to be derived from the Taiji symbol, commonly known in the West as the "Yin-Yang" diagram. "Taiji" means "supreme ultimate force." The concept of Taiji is based on the Taoist philosophy of Yin and Yang, or the attraction of opposites. Yin and Yang combine opposing but complementary forces to create harmony in nature. By using Taiji, a person can bring this principle of harmony into their own life. Some people believe that Tai Chi Quan was developed by Zhang Sanfeng, a Taoist monk from Wudang Mountain. It is said that he once observed a white crane preying on a snake, and mimicked their movements to create the unique Tai Chi Quan.

The main difference between Qigong and Tai Chi Quan is the difference in emphasis. Whether you choose to focus on the breathing of Qigong or the martial arts aspect of Tai Chi Quan, you will find the exercise to be of great value in overall wellness and stress reduction.

Tai Chi Quan's approach of using conscious slow movements is quite different from the typical Western approach to fitness, which often focuses on repetitive movements and physical exertion, such as in fitness regimes like running, biking or weight lifting. Further, "success" in many western sports and athletics is often determined by speed, distance, strength or when competing who "wins". Tai Chi Quan has a completely different set of markers and guideposts for success such as consciousness within body, proper body alignments and developing the smooth flow of energy. It is about generating peace within your entire being. Tai Chi Quan is slow, gentle and doesn't leave the practitioner breathless; it is regarded as no-pain-but-big-gains sport.

Extended Reading 10: Season-based Health Preservation

No matter how you arrange your life, healthy life is a permanent theme. Do you want to know how we Chinese stay healthy? In China, we have a word "Yangsheng" （养生）. It not only is used as a means for people in China to take care of their health, prevent diseases and prolong their life but also embodies the Chinese understanding of life. There is not an equivalent of "Yangsheng" in English, but people in the west have their own way of staying healthy as well as their own understanding of life. With a long history, both Yangsheng in China and staying healthy in the west retain their own features respectively. In 2002 and 2003, a study on the most important factor to prolong the lifespan was conducted among 200 Beijing-ers. It showed that 97.3% think that good mood is the most important, 83.5% favor appropriate exercises and 50% believe in balanced diet. In 2005, the same kind of study was conducted in America. Interestingly, the result shows that 76.67% believe exercise is the most important, 53.33% favor diet and 20% believe in mood.

In China, everything we do is based on two principles: The first is prevention. Prevention is more powerful than cure. To exercise physically and mentally helps the body to maintain its natural Yin and Yang balance by moving the Qi energy and ultimately decreasing the risk of serious illness. The second is wisdom. In modern society too much attention is paid to technology and not enough to wisdom. We believe it is important to abide by natural laws, maintain peace of mind, eat and drink moderately, live a regular life, and never get overstrained so that we can stay healthy.

I. Preserving health in spring

The law of nature is: Sow in spring, grow in summer, harvest in autumn, store in winter（春生，夏长，秋收，冬藏）. And our human bodies should follow the law of nature to prevent illness and preserve health. "To go with it will bring health; to go against it will bring illness."

When spring comes, the temperature rises and the Yang energy increases; all things on earth start to grow. For human bodies, how to preserve health in spring? The main task is to nourish the liver. Spring is liver time; liver is connected to wood, it stores blood, and its indicators are the eyes. This is why during spring, chronic hepatitis plays up, and the eyes become itchy, dry and sleepy. Let me tell you a method. Peel a pear and cut it into pieces. Drip some white vinegar on the pieces, eat them and it will be good for your eyes and liver. Then how to nourish the liver in other ways?

1. Ensure you get enough sleep: This helps the liver cells to function, remove toxins and exchange them for nutrients, and helps the immune system deal with spring viruses.

2. Refresh the spirit: One of the functions of the liver is that it releases emotions to maintain peace of mind, happiness and control over your anger.

3. Have a proper diet: 1) Eat less sour and oily food to help liver energy; 2) Drink lots of water；3) Eat a lot of green vegetables and less meat；4) Drink less alcohol.

4. Take outdoor exercises: 1) The liver's colour is green —go into nature and seek out green colours to help the liver energy. 2) Get up earlier: Because sunrise is Yang energy increasing, getting up when the sun rises will assist your Yang energy in growing.

5. Do feet massage: There are three acupuncture points: Dadun Acupoint（大敦穴）, Xingjian Acupoint（行间穴）and Taichong Acupoint（太冲穴）as the following picture shows. Too much Yang in the liver may lead to toothache, swollen cheek, dental ulcer, nosebleed, etc. Massage the feet from Taichong Acupoint to Xingjian

Acupoint, and the excessive Yang in the liver can be removed from the body.

Dadun Acupoint   Taichong Acupoint   Xingjian Acupoint

In addition, avoiding wind in spring is also important. Spring is a windy season; nature is very wise in using wind to blow away coldness, but on the other hand, people can catch the wind, which causes colds, flu, coughs, asthma, arthritis, and stroke. Because the weather is always changing, it is wise not to remove your clothing too quickly.

II. Preserving health in summer

In the months of summer there is an abundance of sunshine and rain. The Heavenly energy descends and the Earthly energy rises. When these energies merge there is an intimate connection between Heaven and Earth. As a result, plants mature and animals, flowers and fruit appear abundantly. How to preserve our health in summer? Problems in summer will cause injury to the heart and will manifest in fall. In summer, it's hot; people tend to become anxious and lose temper, especially before the thunderstorm, people may have heart-connected problems, such as having a choking sensation in chest, being nervous and in a depressed mood. Then how to protect the heart?

1. Retire later at this time of year while still arising early and exercise properly. During the summer, the best time to exercise outside is in the early morning or late evening.

2. Refrain from anger and stay physically active to keep the skin breathing and to prevent the Qi from stagnating.

3. Eat healthily in summer: 1) Eat some vinegar and ginger. Vinegar can aid digestion and absorption, and appetite. Also, ginger is regarded as one of the best condiments in summer. There is a Chinese saying, "eat radish in winter and ginger in summer." It is believed that it can treat inflammation, and accelerate the circulation of blood. 2) Have some duck meat. Do you know the proper way of cooking it? In China, duck belongs to Yin food (see the note), so it should be baked over the fire, which belongs to Yang. In this way, Yin and Yang are balanced. 3) Take hot tea instead of cold drink. Cold drink makes the stomach contract, resulting in less blood flow as well as less oxygen supply to the digestive system. Combined together, these effects on your body can slow down your digestive system, which gives people the feeling of always having a full stomach.

4. Do hand massage: Clench your fist and the point where the middle finger lies is called Laogong Acupoint（劳宫穴）. Rub the point with the thumb especially in the morning and cover the eyes while the hands are warm. It's good for the heart and eyes. Why do we do it in the morning? Because while we are sleeping, our hearts move slowly; in the morning, we rub the hands in order to help the hearts to move quickly. In this way, illness may be averted in fall.

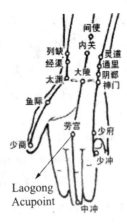

间使
内关
列缺
经渠
灵道
通里
太渊
大陵
阴郄
神门
鱼际
劳宫
少府
少商
少冲
Laogong
Acupoint
中冲

Note: The ideas of Yin and Yang are used in the sphere of food and cooking. Yang foods are believed to increase the body's heat (e.g. raise the metabolism), while Yin foods are believed to decrease the body's heat (e.g. lower the metabolism). As a generalization, Yang foods tend to be dense in food energy, especially energy from fat, while Yin foods tend to have high water content. The Chinese ideal is to eat both types of food to keep the body in balance. A person eating too much Yang food might suffer from acne and bad breath while a person eating too much Yin food might be lethargic or anemic.

III. Preserving health in autumn

In autumn, the law of nature is like this: the Yin energy in the universe increases, the Yang energy begins to fade, temperature drops, wind becomes stronger, and rain gets less. Nature uses these natural phenomena to drive away the wet and humid weather. Dryness in autumn may bring people some discomfort, such as dry skin, sore throat, cough, thirst and other lung problems. So the main task is to battle dryness and nourish the lung. The following are the tips:

1. Get enough sleep: Go to bed early and get up early. A nap of up to an hour at midday is recommended, if you can manage. Getting good quality sleep at Zi (11pm-1am) and Wu (11am-1pm) hours is important for health.

Stay warm: Wear warmer clothes when you go out at night to protect your Yang energy. Close doors and windows to avoid drafts and make sure your tummy is covered and warm.

2. Eat healthily: 1) Eat some sour foods, such as apples, oranges, hawthorn and Kiwi fruit, which help to collect Qi. 2) Eat less spicy foods, such as onions, gingers, which may result in dispersing Qi. 3) Have more white fungus, toufu, honey, and glutinous rice, which help to nourish the lung. 4) Eat more fish, such as hairtail, which can aid digestion and is especially good for those who have dry skin. 5) Eat turnip in the evening. Raw turnip is good for the lung, while cooked turnip can relieve gassy stomach, clear bowels and food retention in stomach. 6) Drink plenty of water and avoid beverages like coffee and tea, which can cause you to lose water.

3. Stay active: 1）Maintaining your physical activity has positive effects on health in fall. It increases your blood circulation, enhances the functions of heart and lung. When the weather supports it, participate in fall activities like hiking, playing Tai Chi Quan, swimming or bike riding. 2）Do rotation practice for the joints: Practice rotation exercise for the major joints every day clockwise and anti clockwise. At the same time, rotate your waist in clockwise and anti-clockwise directions as much as you can comfortably do.

IV. Preserving health in winter

Winter is the coldest season of the year. Humans should follow the law of nature, preserve and store the Yang energy inside their body especially in the kidney. Only if enough Yang energy is preserved and stored in the body, especially in kidney, that sprouting becomes possible in spring, growing in summer and harvest in autumn. What to preserve and store?

1. Preserve and store kidney's essence: TCM holds the view that good preservation and storage of kidney's essence enables the build-up of strong immune system to prevent flu, cold and pollen hypersensitivity in the coming spring. Also the kidney is connected with the bone and produces bone marrow. With a strong kidney's essence, the body and bones would be strong to help prevent dementia, depression, Parkinson's, etc.

2. Preserve and store kidney energy: TCM holds the view that our body has resistance against cold, has good blood circulation system and has energy in the body, with strong Yang energy in the kidney. It also believes that whether a person is ambitious depends on the Yang energy in the kidney. With strong Yang energy in the kidney, one has good memory and clear mind. A person in low spirits or with poor memory is caused by lack of Yang energy in the kidney.

3. Preserve and store the spirit: Seven emotions "excitement, anger, anxiety, sadness, grief, fear, shock" are normal emotions of people. But too much of these emotions would have an adverse effect on the body. Each emotion has a connection with an inner organ. Fear and shock is related to kidney, thus, fear and shock damages the

energy in the kidney, people with weak kidney energy could easily fear or get shocked. Winter is a season to preserve and store kidney's essence and kidney energy, and we must adjust our emotions, especially avoid being affected by fear and shock.

How to preserve and store kidney essence, energy and spirit?

1. Go to bed early and get up late (at the time when the sun rises).

2. Keep warm, especially the lower back (that's near the kidney), abdomen, head, legs and feet. 1) Before going to bed, bathe the feet in hot water of between 55 and 70 degrees centigrade. 2) Warm the kidneys with the back of the hands. Lie on the back and with the back of the hands under the kidneys. The purpose of doing so is to warm the kidneys and drive the coldness in the kidneys out. The best time to do so is between 10:30 pm and 11:00 pm.

3. Do some massage: 1) Massage Qichong Acupoint（气冲穴）at the root of the legs and Yongquan Acupoint（涌泉穴）at the bottom of the feet. 2）Massage the Shenyu Acupoint（肾腧穴）at the back with the back of the fists to stimulate the kidney. 3) Massage hands and feet.

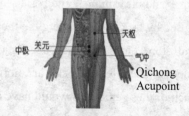

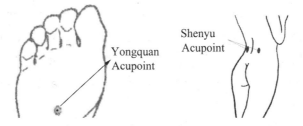

4. Exercise properly: 1）Exercise little fingers, such as using little fingers to lift water, massaging little fingers, or hooking one little finger with another, turning book pages with little fingers. All the ways can be used to enhance the functions of the kidneys. 2) Walking with the knees anticlockwise also helps to nourish the kidney.

5. Eat healthily: 1) Eat warm food, such as porridges and soups, avoid eating and drinking cold food. 2) Eat something bitter, such as oranges, stir-fried livers, vinegar and tea, which helps to nourish heart and enhance the functions of kidney. 3) Eat some meat, beans, and nuts, such as mutton, duck meat, walnuts, sesame, sweet potatoes and turnip.

To sum up, we need to follow the law of nature, have some peace of mind, forget troubles, worries and problems, do some exercises and massage and eat healthily so that we can preserve our health and live long.

9.9 Taoist Music

Taoism music is applied in and indispensable to ceremonious activities. It aims at heightening the religious atmosphere, strengthening followers' belief in immortality and increasing followers' respect for immortals. The vocal music is parted into the Yang tune and the Yin tune. The Yang tune is applied when expressing the hope for longevity and immortality and the Yin tune is applied when praying for the dead.

The Taoist music of Wudang Mountain enjoys a quite long history. During the late stage of the Eastern Han Dynasty, the Five-Dou-Rice Religion came into being. Before long, it was spread from Hanzhong（汉中）in the Shu Kingdom to its neighboring area Wudang Mountain. The ceremony was carried on in a form of singing and dancing by wizards. The ancient wizards entertained the deities or communicated with the dead through singing and dancing to pray for good fortune.

During the period of the Northern and Southern Dynasties, emperors of the Northern Wei Dynasty believed in Taoism. Kou Qianzhi（寇谦之）, a well-known Taoist, launched a reform, changing the Taoist classics-chanting into classics-singing. The movements were extensively spread to Wudang Mountain.

During the periods of Tang and Song Dynasties, more and more influential social activities were held at Wudang Mountain. During the Tang Dynasty (618-907), Yao Jian, an official, prayed for rain at Wudang Mountain and succeeded, then Wudang received great attention. At the same time, some royal family members were degraded and resided in Fangxian and Yunxian counties（房县和郧县）in Wudang Mountain area. The royal music of the Tang Dynasty was then brought to Wudang Mountain.

Chen Tuan in the Five Dynasties was cultured in music. He refined himself at Wudang Mountain for over 20 years and exercised the five-dragon-sleep method. What was special was that there was music while he was sleeping and the music was probably a kind of lullaby. Zhaogou（赵构）, an emperor of the Northern Song Dynasty, summoned Sun Jiran（孙寂然）who was in charge of Wudang Mountain to the imperial palace in Lin' an（临安）to set up an altar and sing classics. It not only took Wudang Taoist music to the royal court, but also brought back the royal court music to Wudang Mountain.

Emperors of the Yuan Dynasty had the greatest esteem for Emperor Zhenwu. The birthday of Emperor Renzong（元仁宗）happened to be on the same day with that of Emperor Zhenwu. Thus, when the day came, a large-scale ceremony was held at Wudang Mountain. After that, holding a sacrificial ceremony for emperor's birthday was an increasing trend; sometimes even four times a year.

In the Qing Dynasty, Wudang Taoism was popular among the folk people. Therefore, making pilgrimage and worshiping in temples became a convention among people in the provinces of Henan, Sichuan, Hubei, Shanxi and some other places. The pilgrimage groups brought folk music of different places to Wudang Mountain; the Taoist music at Wudang Mountain became much more worldly.

(Excerpted from *Mountain Wudang*)

主要参考文献

[1]李发平.《武当山》[M].武汉：湖北人民出版社，2004

[2]陈瑛.《武当山导游词》[M].北京：中国旅游出版社，2011

[3]范学锋.《武当山旅游手册》[M].湖南：湖南地图出版社，2004

[4]魏星.《导游翻译语言修炼》[M].北京：中国旅游出版社，2004

[5]欧阳学忠.《话说武当》[M].北京：中国旅游出版社，2007

[6]谭卫国.《旅游英语的语言特点与翻译》[M].上海：上海交通大学出版社，2007

[7]杨立志.《武当文化概论》[M].北京：社会科学文献出版社，2006

[8]陈刚.《旅游翻译与涉外导游》[M].北京：中国对外翻译出版公司，2004

[9]Eva Wong. *Holding Ying, Embracing Yang* [M]. Boston: Shambhala Publications, Inc., 2007

[10]宋晶.《武当山道教的水文化寓意》[J].理论月刊，2007（12）

[11]宋晶.《武当山天津桥的文化解读》[J].中国道教，2007

（4）

[12]朱歧新.《英语导游必读》[M].北京：中国旅游出版社，2006

后 记

　　自 2005 年起，我院开始招收旅游英语专业的学生。我作为本专业的专业带头人，开始与校内专任教师和校外兼职教师一起共同讨论旅游英语专业的人才培养目标及方案。最终，把"景区涉外导游服务"定为学习领域课程，其中的一个部分就是要求学生们能够针对不同的游客，用英语讲解武当山。这对于我来说，是个难题，更不用说对学生了。

　　每年 11 月或 12 月的时候，本专业有一次淡季景区实习，我系会聘请全国优秀导游刘金燕、芦佳静及其他出色导游来为学生进行武当山示范讲解。但这毕竟是中文的，如何用英语讲解武当山，并且能吸引外国游客的兴趣，需要我们做进一步的研究。为此，我大量阅读了有关武当文化及旅游英语资格翻译的书籍，如杨立志教授著的《武当文化概论》，欧阳学忠主编的《话说武当》，范学锋编著的《武当山旅游手册》，陈刚著的《旅游翻译与涉外导游》，朱歧新编著的《英语导游必读》，丁大刚主编的《旅游英语的语言特点与翻译》，李发平主编的《武当山》，宋晶所写的论文《武当山道教的水文化寓意》、《武当山天津桥的文化解读》，以及 Eva Wong 所著的 *Holding Ying, Embracing Yang* 等国内外学术专著及论文。从这些书籍和资料中，我汲取了营养，找到了自己创作的灵感。

　　在对武当山英文导游辞进行研究与创作的过程中，得到了杨贤玉（湖北汽车工业学院外语系主任、硕士生导师、教授）、吴明清（十堰职业技术学院旅游与涉外事务系前任主任、副教授）、李南峰（十堰职业技术学院原院长助理）、王燕（十堰职业技术学院旅游与涉外事务系现任主任、副教授）、彭家玉（郧阳师专外语系前任系主任、教授）、陈梅（郧阳师专外语系现任系主任、副教授）、刘金燕（武当山地质博物馆主任、全国优秀导游员、十堰职业技术学院旅游专业兼职教师）、芦佳静（武当山特区政府接待办公室、全国优秀导游员、十堰职业技术学院旅游专业兼职教师）、张挺（武当山道源文化发展有限公司法人、英文导游、十堰职业技术学院旅游英语专业兼职教师）、邓丽（十堰职业技术学院旅游与涉外事务系副主任、中级英文导游）、喻富明（武当山中学高级英语教师、英文导游）、来我院从事教学的历任外教 Rena, Jeremy, Megan, John 和 David，以及美国游客 Aaron, Todd 等国内外专家的大力帮助，在此一并表示感谢！

张正荣

2012 年 12 月